Myths and Legends of the Sioux

Myths and Legends of the Sioux

Marie L. McLaughlin

MINT EDITIONS

Myths and Legends of the Sioux was first published in 1916.

This edition published by Mint Editions 2021.

ISBN 9781513277462 | E-ISBN 9781513277875

Published by Mint Editions®

MINT
EDITIONS
minteditionbooks.com

Publishing Director: Jennifer Newens
Design & Production: Rachel Lopez Metzger
Project Manager: Micaela Clark
Typesetting: Westchester Publishing Services

Contents

Foreword   9

The Forgotten Ear of Corn   11

The Little Mice   12

The Pet Rabbit   13

The Pet Donkey   14

The Rabbit and the Elk   16

The Rabbit and the Grouse Girls   17

The Faithful Lovers   18

The Artichoke and the Muskrat   22

The Rabbit and the Bear with the Flint Body   23

Story of the Lost Wife   25

The Raccoon and the Crawfish   27

Legend of Standing Rock   28

Story of the Peace Pipe   29

A Bashful Courtship   30

The Simpleton's Wisdom   31

A Little Brave and the Medicine Woman   33

The Bound Children   35

The Signs of Corn 39

Story of the Rabbits 41

How the Rabbit Lost his Tail 42

Unktomi and the Arrowheads 47

The Bear and the Rabbit Hunt Buffalo 49

The Brave Who Went on the Warpath Alone
    and Won the Name of the Lone Warrior 52

The Sioux Who Married the Crow Chief's Daughter 57

The Boy and the Turtles 60

The Hermit, or the Gift of Corn 62

The Mysterious Butte 64

The Wonderful Turtle 66

The Man and the Oak 68

Story of the Two Young Friends 71

The Story of the Pet Crow 81

The "Wasna" (Pemmican Man)
    and the Unktomi (Spider) 84

The Resuscitation of the Only Daughter 86

The Story of the Pet Crane 90

White Plume 93

Story of Pretty Feathered Forehead 101

The Four Brothers or Inyanhoksila (Stone Boy)   106

The Unktomi (Spider), Two Widows
    and the Red Plums   117

Foreword

In publishing these "Myths of the Sioux," I deem it proper to state that I am of one-fourth Sioux blood. My maternal grandfather, Captain Duncan Graham, a Scotchman by birth, who had seen service in the British Army, was one of a party of Scotch Highlanders who in 1811 arrived in the British Northwest by way of York Factory, Hudson Bay, to found what was known as the Selkirk Colony, near Lake Winnipeg, now within the province of Manitoba, Canada. Soon after his arrival at Lake Winnipeg he proceeded up the Red River of the North and the western fork thereof to its source, and thence down the Minnesota River to Mendota, the confluence of the Minnesota and Mississippi Rivers, where he located. My grandmother, Ha-za-ho-ta-win, was a full-blood of the Medawakanton Band of the Sioux Tribe of Indians. My father, Joseph Buisson, born near Montreal, Canada, was connected with the American Fur Company, with headquarters at Mendota, Minnesota, which point was for many years the chief distributing depot of the American Fur Company, from which the Indian trade conducted by that company on the upper Mississippi was directed.

I was born December 8, 1842, at Wabasha, Minnesota, then Indian country, and resided thereat until fourteen years of age, when I was sent to school at Prairie du Chien, Wisconsin.

I was married to Major James McLaughlin at Mendota, Minnesota, January 28, 1864, and resided in Minnesota until July 1, 1871, when I accompanied my husband to Devils Lake Agency, North Dakota, then Dakota Territory, where I remained ten years in most friendly relations with the Indians of that agency. My husband was Indian agent at Devils Lake Agency, and in 1881 was transferred to Standing Rock, on the Missouri River, then a very important agency, to take charge of the Sioux who had then but recently surrendered to the military authorities, and been brought by steamboat from various points on the upper Missouri, to be permanently located on the Standing Rock reservation.

Having been born and reared in an Indian community, I at an early age acquired a thorough knowledge of the Sioux language, and having lived on Indian reservations for the past forty years in a position which brought me very near to the Indians, whose confidence I possessed, I have, therefore, had exceptional opportunities of learning the legends and folk-lore of the Sioux.

The stories contained in this little volume were told me by the older men and women of the Sioux, of which I made careful notes as related, knowing that, if not recorded, these fairy tales would be lost to posterity by the passing of the primitive Indian.

The notes of a song or a strain of music coming to us through the night not only give us pleasure by the melody they bring, but also give us knowledge of the character of the singer or of the instrument from which they proceed. There is something in the music which unerringly tells us of its source. I believe musicians call it the "timbre" of the sound. It is independent of, and different from, both pitch and rhythm; it is the texture of the music itself.

The "timbre" of a people's stories tells of the qualities of that people's heart. It is the texture of the thought, independent of its form or fashioning, which tells the quality of the mind from which it springs.

In the "timbre" of these stories of the Sioux, told in the lodges and at the camp fires of the past, and by the firesides of the Dakotas of today, we recognize the very texture of the thought of a simple, grave, and sincere people, living in intimate contact and friendship with the big out-of-doors that we call Nature; a race not yet understanding all things, not proud and boastful, but honest and childlike and fair; a simple, sincere, and gravely thoughtful people, willing to believe that there may be in even the everyday things of life something not yet fully understood; a race that can, without any loss of native dignity, gravely consider the simplest things, seeking to fathom their meaning and to learn their lesson—equally without vain-glorious boasting and trifling cynicism; an earnest, thoughtful, dignified, but simple and primitive people.

To the children of any race these stories can not fail to give pleasure by their vivid imaging of the simple things and creatures of the great out-of-doors and the epics of their doings. They will also give an intimate insight into the mentality of an interesting race at a most interesting stage of development, which is now fast receding into the mists of the past.

MARIE L. McLAUGHLIN (Mrs. James McLaughlin)
McLaughlin, S. D., May 1, 1913.

The Forgotten Ear of Corn

An Arikara woman was once gathering corn from the field to store away for winter use. She passed from stalk to stalk, tearing off the ears and dropping them into her folded robe. When all was gathered she started to go, when she heard a faint voice, like a child's, weeping and calling:

"Oh, do not leave me! Do not go away without me."

The woman was astonished. "What child can that be?" she asked herself. "What babe can be lost in the cornfield?"

She set down her robe in which she had tied up her corn, and went back to search; but she found nothing.

As she started away she heard the voice again:

"Oh, do not leave me. Do not go away without me."

She searched for a long time. At last in one corner of the field, hidden under the leaves of the stalks, she found one little ear of corn. This it was that had been crying, and this is why all Indian women have since garnered their corn crop very carefully, so that the succulent food product should not even to the last small nubbin be neglected or wasted, and thus displease the Great Mystery.

THE LITTLE MICE

Once upon a time a prairie mouse busied herself all fall storing away a cache of beans. Every morning she was out early with her empty cast-off snake skin, which she filled with ground beans and dragged home with her teeth.

The little mouse had a cousin who was fond of dancing and talk, but who did not like to work. She was not careful to get her cache of beans and the season was already well gone before she thought to bestir herself. When she came to realize her need, she found she had no packing bag. So she went to her hardworking cousin and said:

"Cousin, I have no beans stored for winter and the season is nearly gone. But I have no snake skin to gather the beans in. Will you lend me one?"

"But why have you no packing bag? Where were you in the moon when the snakes cast off their skins?"

"I was here."

"What were you doing?"

"I was busy talking and dancing."

"And now you are punished," said the other. "It is always so with lazy, careless people. But I will let you have the snake skin. And now go, and by hard work and industry, try to recover your wasted time."

The Pet Rabbit

A little girl owned a pet rabbit which she loved dearly. She carried it on her back like a babe, made for it a little pair of moccasins, and at night shared with it her own robe.

Now the little girl had a cousin who loved her very dearly and wished to do her honor; so her cousin said to herself:

"I love my little cousin well and will ask her to let me carry her pet rabbit around;" (for thus do Indian women when they wish to honor a friend; they ask permission to carry about the friend's babe).

She then went to the little girl and said:

"Cousin, let me carry your pet rabbit about on my back. Thus shall I show you how I love you."

Her mother, too, said to her: "Oh no, do not let our little grandchild go away from our tepee."

But the cousin answered: "Oh, do let me carry it. I do so want to show my cousin honor." At last they let her go away with the pet rabbit on her back.

When the little girl's cousin came home to her tepee, some rough boys who were playing about began to make sport of her. To tease the little girl they threw stones and sticks at the pet rabbit. At last a stick struck the little rabbit upon the head and killed it.

When her pet was brought home dead, the little rabbit's adopted mother wept bitterly. She cut off her hair for mourning and all her little girl friends wailed with her. Her mother, too, mourned with them.

"Alas!" they cried, "alas, for the little rabbit. He was always kind and gentle. Now your child is dead and you will be lonesome."

The little girl's mother called in her little friends and made a great mourning feast for the little rabbit. As he lay in the tepee his adopted mother's little friends brought many precious things and covered his body. At the feast were given away robes and kettles and blankets and knives and great wealth in honor of the little rabbit. Him they wrapped in a robe with his little moccasins on and buried him in a high place upon a scaffold.

The Pet Donkey

There was a chief's daughter once who had a great many relations so that everybody knew she belonged to a great family.

When she grew up she married and there were born to her twin sons. This caused great rejoicing in her father's camp, and all the village women came to see the babes. She was very happy.

As the babes grew older, their grandmother made for them two saddle bags and brought out a donkey.

"My two grandchildren," said the old lady, "shall ride as is becoming to children having so many relations. Here is this donkey. He is patient and surefooted. He shall carry the babes in the saddle bags, one on either side of his back."

It happened one day that the chief's daughter and her husband were making ready to go on a camping journey. The father, who was quite proud of his children, brought out his finest pony, and put the saddle bags on the pony's back.

"There," he said, "my sons shall ride on the pony, not on a donkey; let the donkey carry the pots and kettles."

So his wife loaded the donkey with the household things. She tied the tepee poles into two great bundles, one on either side of the donkey's back; across them she put the travois net and threw into it the pots and kettles and laid the skin tent across the donkey's back.

But no sooner done than the donkey began to rear and bray and kick. He broke the tent poles and kicked the pots and kettles into bits and tore the skin tent. The more he was beaten the more he kicked.

At last they told the grandmother. She laughed. "Did I not tell you the donkey was for the children," she cried. "He knows the babies are the chief's children. Think you he will be dishonored with pots and kettles?" and she fetched the children and slung them over the donkey's back, when he became at once quiet again.

The camping party left the village and went on their journey. But the next day as they passed by a place ovfootnergrown with bushes, a band of enemies rushed out, lashing their ponies and sounding their war whoop. All was excitement. The men bent their bows and seized their lances. After a long battle the enemy fled. But when the camping party came together again—where were the donkey and the two babes? No one knew. For a long time they searched, but in vain. At last they turned to go back to the village, the father mournful, the mother wailing. When they came to the grandmother's tepee, there stood the good donkey with the two babes in the saddle bags.

The Rabbit and the Elk

The little rabbit lived with his old grandmother, who needed a new dress. "I will go out and trap a deer or an elk for you," he said. "Then you shall have a new dress."

When he went out hunting he laid down his bow in the path while he looked at his snares. An elk coming by saw the bow.

"I will play a joke on the rabbit," said the elk to himself. "I will make him think I have been caught in his bow string." He then put one foot on the string and lay down as if dead.

By and by the rabbit returned. When he saw the elk he was filled with joy and ran home crying: "Grandmother, I have trapped a fine elk. You shall have a new dress from his skin. Throw the old one in the fire!"

This the old grandmother did.

The elk now sprang to his feet laughing. "Ho, friend rabbit," he called, "You thought to trap me; now I have mocked you." And he ran away into the thicket.

The rabbit who had come back to skin the elk now ran home again. "Grandmother, don't throw your dress in the fire," he cried. But it was too late. The old dress was burned.

The Rabbit and the Grouse Girls

The rabbit once went out on the prairie in winter time. On the side of a hill away from the wind he found a great company of girls all with grey and speckled blankets over their backs. They were the grouse girls and they were coasting down hill on a board. When the rabbit saw them, he called out:

"Oh, maidens, that is not a good way to coast down hill. Let me get you a fine skin with bangles on it that tinkle as you slide." And away he ran to the tepee and brought a skin bag. It had red stripes on it and bangles that tinkled. "Come and get inside," he said to the grouse girls. "Oh, no, we are afraid," they answered. "Don't be afraid, I can't hurt you. Come, one of you," said the rabbit. Then as each hung back he added coaxingly: "If each is afraid alone, come all together. I can't hurt you *all*." And so he coaxed the whole flock into the bag. This done, the rabbit closed the mouth of the bag, slung it over his back and came home. "Grandmother," said he, as he came to the tepee, "here is a bag full of game. Watch it while I go for willow sticks to make spits."

But as soon as the rabbit had gone out of the tent, the grouse girls began to cry out:

"Grandmother, let us out."

"Who are you?" asked the old woman.

"Your dear grandchildren," they answered.

"But how came you in the bag?" asked the old woman.

"Oh, our cousin was jesting with us. He coaxed us in the bag for a joke. Please let us out."

"Certainly, dear grandchildren, I will let you out," said the old woman as she untied the bag: and lo, the grouse flock with achuck-a-chuck-achuck flew up, knocking over the old grandmother and flew out of the square smoke opening of the winter lodge. The old woman caught only one grouse as it flew up and held it, grasping a leg with each hand.

When the rabbit came home with the spits she called out to him:

"Grandson, come quick. They got out but I have caught two."

When he saw what had happened he was quite angry, yet could not keep from laughing.

"Grandmother, you have but one grouse," he cried, "and it is a very skinny one at that."

THE FAITHFUL LOVERS

There once lived a chief's daughter who had many relations. All the young men in the village wanted to have her for wife, and were all eager to fill her skin bucket when she went to the brook for water.

There was a young man in the village who was industrious and a good hunter; but he was poor and of a mean family. He loved the maiden and when she went for water, he threw his robe over her head while he whispered in her ear:

"Be my wife. I have little but I am young and strong. I will treat you well, for I love you."

For a long time the maiden did not answer, but one day she whispered back.

"Yes, you may ask my father's leave to marry me. But first you must do something noble. I belong to a great family and have many relations. You must go on a war party and bring back the scalp of an enemy."

The young man answered modestly, "I will try to do as you bid me. I am only a hunter, not a warrior. Whether I shall be brave or not I do not know. But I will try to take a scalp for your sake."

So he made a war party of seven, himself and six other young men. They wandered through the enemy's country, hoping to get a chance to strike a blow. But none came, for they found no one of the enemy.

"Our medicine is unfavorable," said their leader at last. "We shall have to return home."

Before they started they sat down to smoke and rest beside a beautiful lake at the foot of a green knoll that rose from its shore. The knoll was covered with green grass and somehow as they looked at it they had a feeling that there was something about it that was mysterious or uncanny.

But there was a young man in the party named the jester, for he was venturesome and full of fun. Gazing at the knoll he said: "Let's run and jump on its top."

"No," said the young lover, "it looks mysterious. Sit still and finish your smoke."

"Oh, come on, who's afraid," said the jester, laughing. "Come on you—come on!" and springing to his feet he ran up the side of the knoll.

Four of the young men followed. Having reached the top of the knoll all five began to jump and stamp about in sport, calling, "Come on, come on," to the others. Suddenly they stopped—the knoll had begun to move toward the water. It was a gigantic turtle. The five men cried out in alarm and tried to run—too late! Their feet by some power were held fast to the monster's back.

"Help us—drag us away," they cried; but the others could do nothing. In a few moments the waves had closed over them.

The other two men, the lover and his friend, went on, but with heavy hearts, for they had forebodings of evil. After some days, they came to a river. Worn with fatigue the lover threw himself down on the bank.

"I will sleep awhile," he said, "for I am wearied and worn out."

"And I will go down to the water and see if I can chance upon a dead fish. At this time of the year the high water may have left one stranded on the seashore," said his friend.

And as he had said, he found a fish which he cleaned, and then called to the lover.

"Come and eat the fish with me. I have cleaned it and made a fire and it is now cooking."

"No, you eat it; let me rest," said the lover.

"Oh, come on."

"No, let me rest."

"But you are my friend. I will not eat unless you share it with me."

"Very well," said the lover, "I will eat the fish with you, but you must first make me a promise. If I eat the fish, you must promise, pledge yourself, to fetch me all the water that I can drink."

"I promise," said the other, and the two ate the fish out of their war-kettle. For there had been but one kettle for the party.

When they had eaten, the kettle was rinsed out and the lover's friend brought it back full of water. This the lover drank at a draught.

"Bring me more," he said.

Again his friend filled the kettle at the river and again the lover drank it dry.

"More!" he cried.

"Oh, I am tired. Cannot you go to the river and drink your fill from the stream?" asked his friend.

"Remember your promise."

"Yes, but I am weary. Go now and drink."

"Ek-hey, I feared it would be so. Now trouble is coming upon us," said the lover sadly. He walked to the river, sprang in, and lying down in the water with his head toward land, drank greedily. By and by he called to his friend.

"Come hither, you who have been my sworn friend. See what comes of your broken promise."

The friend came and was amazed to see that the lover was now a fish from his feet to his middle.

Sick at heart he ran off a little way and threw himself upon the ground in grief. By and by he returned. The lover was now a fish to his neck.

"Cannot I cut off the part and restore you by a sweat bath?" the friend asked.

"No, it is too late. But tell the chief's daughter that I loved her to the last and that I die for her sake. Take this belt and give it to her. She gave it to me as a pledge of her love for me," and he being then turned to a great fish, swam to the middle of the river and there remained, only his great fin remaining above the water.

The friend went home and told his story. There was great mourning over the death of the five young men, and for the lost lover. In the river the great fish remained, its fin just above the surface, and was called by the Indians "Fish that Bars," because it bar'd navigation. Canoes had to be portaged at great labor around the obstruction.

The chief's daughter mourned for her lover as for a husband, nor would she be comforted. "He was lost for love of me, and I shall remain as his widow," she wailed.

In her mother's tepee she sat, with her head covered with her robe, silent, working, working. "What is my daughter doing," her mother asked. But the maiden did not reply.

The days lengthened into moons until a year had passed. And then the maiden arose. In her hands were beautiful articles of clothing, enough for three men. There were three pairs of moccasins, three pairs of leggings, three belts, three shirts, three head dresses with beautiful feathers, and sweet smelling tobacco.

"Make a new canoe of bark," she said, which was made for her.

Into the canoe she stepped and floated slowly down the river toward the great fish.

"Come back my daughter," her mother cried in agony. "Come back. The great fish will eat you."

She answered nothing. Her canoe came to the place where the great fin arose and stopped, its prow grating on the monster's back.

The maiden stepped out boldly. One by one she laid her presents on the fish's back, scattering the feathers and tobacco over his broad spine.

"Oh, fish," she cried, "Oh, fish, you who were my lover, I shall not forget you. Because you were lost for love of me, I shall never marry. All my life I shall remain a widow. Take these presents. And now leave the river, and let the waters run free, so my people may once more descend in their canoes."

She stepped into her canoe and waited. Slowly the great fish sank, his broad fin disappeared, and the waters of the St. Croix (Stillwater) were free.

The Artichoke and the Muskrat

O n the shore of a lake stood an artichoke with its green leaves waving in the sun. Very proud of itself it was, and well satisfied with the world. In the lake below lived a muskrat in his tepee, and in the evening as the sun set he would come out upon the shore and wander over the bank. One evening he came near the place where the artichoke stood.

"Ho, friend," he said, "you seem rather proud of yourself. Who are you?" "I am the artichoke," answered the other, "and I have many handsome cousins. But who are you?"

"I am the muskrat, and I, too, belong to a large family. I live in the water. I don't stand all day in one place like a stone."

"If I stand in one place all day," retorted the artichoke, "at least I don't swim around in stagnant water, and build my lodge in the mud."

"You are jealous of my fine fur," sneered the muskrat. "I may build my lodge in the mud, but I always have a clean coat. But you are half buried in the ground, and when men dig you up, you are never clean."

"And your fine coat always smells of musk," jeered the artichoke.

"That is true," said the muskrat. "But men think well of me, nevertheless. They trap me for the fine sinew in my tail; and handsome young women bite off my tail with their white teeth and make it into thread."

"That's nothing," laughed the artichoke. "Handsome young warriors, painted and splendid with feathers, dig me up, brush me off with their shapely hands and eat me without even taking the trouble to wash me off."

The Rabbit and the Bear with the Flint Body

The Rabbit and his grandmother were in dire straits, because the rabbit was out of arrows. The fall hunt would soon be on and his quiver was all but empty. Arrow sticks he could cut in plenty, but he had nothing with which to make arrowheads.

"You must make some flint arrowheads," said his grandmother. "Then you will be able to kill game."

"Where shall I get the flint?" asked the rabbit.

"From the old bear chief," said his old grandmother. For at that time all the flint in the world was in the bear's body.

So the rabbit set out for the village of the Bears. It was winter time and the lodges of the bears were set under the shelter of a hill where the cold wind would not blow on them and where they had shelter among the trees and bushes.

He came at one end of the village to a hut where lived an old woman. He pushed open the door and entered. Everybody who came for flint always stopped there because it was the first lodge on the edge of the village. Strangers were therefore not unusual in the old woman's hut, and she welcomed the rabbit. She gave him a seat and at night he lay with his feet to the fire.

The next morning the rabbit went to the lodge of the bear chief. They sat together awhile and smoked. At last the bear chief spoke.

"What do you want, my grandson?"

"I have come for some flint to make arrows," answered the rabbit.

The bear chief grunted, and laid aside his pipe. Leaning back he pulled off his robe and, sure enough, one half of his body was flesh and the other half hard flint.

"Bring a stone hammer and give it to our guest," he bade his wife. Then as the rabbit took the hammer he said: "Do not strike too hard."

"Grandfather, I shall be careful," said the rabbit. With a stroke he struck off a little flake of flint from the bear's body.

"Ni-sko-ke-cha? So big?" he asked.

"Harder, grandson; strike off bigger pieces," said the bear.

The rabbit struck a little harder.

"Ni-sko-ke-cha? So big?" he asked.

The bear grew impatient. "No, no, strike off bigger pieces. I can't be here all day. Tanka kaksa wo! Break off a big piece."

The rabbit struck again—hard! "Ni-sko-ke-cha?" he cried, as the hammer fell. But even as he spoke the bear's body broke in two, the flesh part fell away and only the flint part remained. Like a flash the rabbit darted out of the hut.

There was a great outcry in the village. Openmouthed, all the bears gave chase. But as he ran the rabbit cried: "Wa-hin-han-yo (snow, snow) Ota-po, Ota-po—lots more, lots more," and a great storm of snow swept down from the sky.

The rabbit, light of foot, bounded over the top of the snow. The bears sunk in and floundered about helpless. Seeing this, the rabbit turned back and killed them one by one with his club. That is why we now have so few bears.

Story of the Lost Wife

A Dakota girl married a man who promised to treat her kindly, but he did not keep his word. He was unreasonable, fault-finding, and often beat her. Frantic with his cruelty, she ran away. The whole village turned out to search for her, but no trace of the missing wife was to be found.

Meanwhile, the fleeing woman had wandered about all that day and the next night. The next day she met a man, who asked her who she was. She did not know it, but he was not really a man, but the chief of the wolves.

"Come with me," he said, and he led her to a large village. She was amazed to see here many wolves—gray and black, timber wolves and coyotes. It seemed as if all the wolves in the world were there.

The wolf chief led the young woman to a great tepee and invited her in. He asked her what she ate for food.

"Buffalo meat," she answered.

He called two coyotes and bade them bring what the young woman wanted. They bounded away and soon returned with the shoulder of a fresh-killed buffalo calf.

"How do you prepare it for eating?" asked the wolf chief.

"By boiling," answered the young woman.

Again he called the two coyotes. Away they bounded and soon brought into the tent a small bundle. In it were punk, flint and steel—stolen, it may be, from some camp of men.

"How do you make the meat ready?" asked the wolf chief.

"I cut it into slices," answered the young woman.

The coyotes were called and in a short time fetched in a knife in its sheath. The young woman cut up the calf's shoulder into slices and ate it.

Thus she lived for a year, all the wolves being very kind to her. At the end of that time the wolf chief said to her:

"Your people are going off on a buffalo hunt. Tomorrow at noon they will be here. You must then go out and meet them or they will fall on us and kill us."

The next day at about noon the young woman went to the top of a neighboring knoll. Coming toward her were some young men riding on their ponies. She stood up and held her hands so that they could see her. They wondered who she was, and when they were close by gazed at her closely.

"A year ago we lost a young woman; if you are she, where have you been," they asked.

"I have been in the wolves' village. Do not harm them," she answered.

"We will ride back and tell the people," they said. "Tomorrow again at noon, we shall meet you."

The young woman went back to the wolf village, and the next day went again to a neighboring knoll, though to a different one. Soon she saw the camp coming in a long line over the prairie. First were the warriors, then the women and tents.

The young woman's father and mother were overjoyed to see her. But when they came near her the young woman fainted, for she could not now bear the smell of human kind. When she came to herself she said:

"You must go on a buffalo hunt, my father and all the hunters. Tomorrow you must come again, bringing with you the tongues and choice pieces of the kill."

This he promised to do; and all the men of the camp mounted their ponies and they had a great hunt. The next day they returned with their ponies laden with the buffalo meat. The young woman bade them pile the meat in a great heap between two hills which she pointed out to them. There was so much meat that the tops of the two hills were bridged level between by the meat pile. In the center of the pile the young woman planted a pole with a red flag. She then began to howl like a wolf, loudly.

In a moment the earth seemed covered with wolves. They fell greedily on the meat pile and in a short time had eaten the last scrap.

The young woman then joined her own people.

Her husband wanted her to come and live with him again. For a long time she refused. However, at last they became reconciled.

The Raccoon and the Crawfish

S harp and cunning is the raccoon, say the Indians, by whom he is named Spotted Face.

A crawfish one evening wandered along a river bank, looking for something dead to feast upon. A raccoon was also out looking for something to eat. He spied the crawfish and formed a plan to catch him.

He lay down on the bank and feigned to be dead. By and by the crawfish came near by. "Ho," he thought, "here is a feast indeed; but is he really dead. I will go near and pinch him with my claws and find out."

So he went near and pinched the raccoon on the nose and then on his soft paws. The raccoon never moved. The crawfish then pinched him on the ribs and tickled him so that the raccoon could hardly keep from laughing. The crawfish at last left him. "The raccoon is surely dead," he thought. And he hurried back to the crawfish village and reported his find to the chief.

All the villagers were called to go down to the feast. The chief bade the warriors and young men to paint their faces and dress in their gayest for a dance.

So they marched in a long line—first the warriors, with their weapons in hand, then the women with their babies and children—to the place where the raccoon lay. They formed a great circle about him and danced, singing:

"We shall have a great feast

"On the spotted-faced beast, with soft smooth paws:

"He is dead!

"He is dead!

"We shall dance!

"We shall have a good time!

"We shall feast on his flesh."

But as they danced, the raccoon suddenly sprang to his feet.

"Who is that you say you are going to eat? He has a spotted face, has he? He has soft, smooth paws, has he? I'll break your ugly backs. I'll break your rough bones. I'll crunch your ugly, rough paws." And he rushed among the crawfish, killing them by scores. The crawfish warriors fought bravely and the women ran screaming, all to no purpose. They did not feast on the raccoon; the raccoon feasted *on them!*

Legend of Standing Rock

A Dakota had married an Arikara woman, and by her had one child. By and by he took another wife. The first wife was jealous and pouted. When time came for the village to break camp she refused to move from her place on the tent floor. The tent was taken down but she sat on the ground with her babe on her back The rest of the camp with her husband went on.

At noon her husband halted the line. "Go back to your sister-in-law," he said to his two brothers. "Tell her to come on and we will await you here. But hasten, for I fear she may grow desperate and kill herself."

The two rode off and arrived at their former camping place in the evening. The woman still sat on the ground. The elder spoke:

"Sister-in-law, get up. We have come for you. The camp awaits you."

She did not answer, and he put out his hand and touched her head. She had turned to stone!

The two brothers lashed their ponies and came back to camp. They told their story, but were not believed. "The woman has killed herself and my brothers will not tell me," said the husband. However, the whole village broke camp and came back to the place where they had left the woman. Sure enough, she sat there still, a block of stone.

The Indians were greatly excited. They chose out a handsome pony, made a new travois and placed the stone in the carrying net. Pony and travois were both beautifully painted and decorated with streamers and colors. The stone was thought *"wakan"* (holy), and was given a place of honor in the center of the camp. Whenever the camp moved the stone and travois were taken along. Thus the stone woman was carried for years, and finally brought to Standing Rock Agency, and now rests upon a brick pedestal in front of the Agency office. From this stone Standing Rock Agency derives its name.

Story of the Peace Pipe

Two young men were out strolling one night talking of love affairs. They passed around a hill and came to a little ravine or coulee. Suddenly they saw coming up from the ravine a beautiful woman. She was painted and her dress was of the very finest material.

"What a beautiful girl!" said one of the young men. "Already I love her. I will steal her and make her my wife."

"No," said the other. "Don't harm her. She may be holy."

The young woman approached and held out a pipe which she first offered to the sky, then to the earth and then advanced, holding it out in her extended hands.

"I know what you young men have been saying; one of you is good; the other is wicked," she said.

She laid down the pipe on the ground and at once became a buffalo cow. The cow pawed the ground, stuck her tail straight out behind her and then lifted the pipe from the ground again in her hoofs; immediately she became a young woman again.

"I am come to give you this gift," she said. "It is the peace pipe. Hereafter all treaties and ceremonies shall be performed after smoking it. It shall bring peaceful thoughts into your minds. You shall offer it to the Great Mystery and to mother earth."

The two young men ran to the village and told what they had seen and heard. All the village came out where the young woman was.

She repeated to them what she had already told the young men and added:

"When you set free the ghost (the spirit of deceased persons) you must have a white buffalo cow skin."

She gave the pipe to the medicine men of the village, turned again to a buffalo cow and fled away to the land of buffaloes.

A Bashful Courtship

A young man lived with his grandmother. He was a good hunter and wished to marry. He knew a girl who was a good moccasin maker, but she belonged to a great family. He wondered how he could win her.

One day she passed the tent on her way to get water at the river. His grandmother was at work in the tepee with a pair of old worn-out sloppy moccasins. The young man sprang to his feet. "Quick, grandmother— let me have those old sloppy moccasins you have on your feet!" he cried.

"My old moccasins, what do you want of them?" cried the astonished woman.

"Never mind! Quick! I can't stop to talk," answered the grandson as he caught up the old moccasins the old lady had doffed, and put them on. He threw a robe over his shoulders, slipped through the door, and hastened to the watering place. The girl had just arrived with her bucket.

"Let me fill your bucket for you," said the young man.

"Oh, no, I can do it."

"Oh, let me, I can go in the mud. You surely don't want to soil your moccasins," and taking the bucket he slipped in the mud, taking care to push his sloppy old moccasins out so the girl could see them. She giggled outright.

"My, what old moccasins you have," she cried.

"Yes, I have nobody to make me a new pair," he answered.

"Why don't you get your grandmother to make you a new pair?"

"She's old and blind and can't make them any longer. That's why I want you," he answered.

"Oh, you're fooling me. You aren't speaking the truth."

"Yes, I am. If you don't believe—come with me *now!*"

The girl looked down; so did the youth. At last he said softly:

"Well, which is it? Shall I take up your bucket, or will you go with me?"

And she answered, still more softly: "I guess I'll go with you!"

The girl's aunt came down to the river, wondering what kept her niece so long. In the mud she found two pairs of moccasin tracks close together; at the edge of the water stood an empty keg.

THE SIMPLETON'S WISDOM

There was a man and his wife who had one daughter. Mother and daughter were deeply attached to one another, and when the latter died the mother was disconsolate. She cut off her hair, cut gashes in her cheeks and sat before the corpse with her robe drawn over her head, mourning for her dead. Nor would she let them touch the body to take it to a burying scaffold. She had a knife in her hand, and if anyone offered to come near the body the mother would wail:

"I am weary of life. I do not care to live. I will stab myself with this knife and join my daughter in the land of spirits."

Her husband and relatives tried to get the knife from her, but could not. They feared to use force lest she kill herself. They came together to see what they could do.

"We must get the knife away from her," they said.

At last they called a boy, a kind of simpleton, yet with a good deal of natural shrewdness. He was an orphan and very poor. His moccasins were out at the sole and he was dressed in wei-zi (coarse buffalo skin, smoked).

"Go to the tepee of the mourning mother," they told the simpleton, "and in some way contrive to make her laugh and forget her grief. Then try to get the knife away from her."

The boy went to the tent and sat down at the door as if waiting to be given something. The corpse lay in the place of honor where the dead girl had slept in life. The body was wrapped in a rich robe and wrapped about with ropes. Friends had covered it with rich offerings out of respect to the dead.

As the mother sat on the ground with her head covered she did not at first see the boy, who sat silent. But when his reserve had worn away a little he began at first lightly, then more heavily, to drum on the floor with his hands. After a while he began to sing a comic song. Louder and louder he sang until carried away with his own singing he sprang up and began to dance, at the same time gesturing and making all manner of contortions with his body, still singing the comic song. As he approached the corpse he waved his hands over it in blessing. The mother put her head out of the blanket and when she saw the poor simpleton with his strange grimaces trying to do honor to the corpse by his solemn waving, and at the same time keeping up his comic song, she burst out laughing. Then she reached over and handed her knife to the simpleton.

"Take this knife," she said. "You have taught me to forget my grief. If while I mourn for the dead I can still be mirthful, there is no reason for me to despair. I no longer care to die. I will live for my husband."

The simpleton left the tepee and brought the knife to the astonished husband and relatives.

"How did you get it? Did you force it away from her, or did you steal it?" they said.

"She gave it to me. How could I force it from her or steal it when she held it in her hand, blade uppermost? I sang and danced for her and she burst out laughing. Then she gave it to me," he answered.

When the old men of the village heard the orphan's story they were very silent. It was a strange thing for a lad to dance in a tepee where there was mourning. It was stranger that a mother should laugh in a tepee before the corpse of her dead daughter. The old men gathered at last in a council. They sat a long time without saying anything, for they did not want to decide hastily. The pipe was filled and passed many times. At last an old man spoke.

"We have a hard question. A mother has laughed before the corpse of her daughter, and many think she has done foolishly, but I think the woman did wisely. The lad was simple and of no training, and we cannot expect him to know how to do as well as one with good home and parents to teach him. Besides, he did the best that he knew. He danced to make the mother forget her grief, and he tried to honor the corpse by waving over it his hands."

"The mother did right to laugh, for when one does try to do us good, even if what he does causes us discomfort, we should always remember rather the motive than the deed. And besides, the simpleton's dancing saved the woman's life, for she gave up her knife. In this, too, she did well, for it is always better to live for the living than to die for the dead."

A Little Brave and
the Medicine Woman

A village of Indians moved out of winter camp and pitched their tents in a circle on high land overlooking a lake. A little way down the declivity was a grave. Choke cherries had grown up, hiding the grave from view. But as the ground had sunk somewhat, the grave was marked by a slight hollow.

One of the villagers going out to hunt took a short cut through the choke cherry bushes. As he pushed them aside he saw the hollow grave, but thought it was a washout made by the rains. But as he essayed to step over it, to his great surprise he stumbled and fell. Made curious by his mishap, he drew back and tried again; but again he fell. When he came back to the village he told the old men what had happened to him. They remembered then that a long time before there had been buried there a medicine woman or conjurer. Doubtless it was her medicine that made him stumble.

The story of the villager's adventure spread thru the camp and made many curious to see the grave. Among others were six little boys who were, however, rather timid, for they were in great awe of the dead medicine woman. But they had a little playmate named Brave, a mischievous little rogue, whose hair was always unkempt and tossed about and who was never quiet for a moment.

"Let us ask Brave to go with us," they said; and they went in a body to see him.

"All right," said Brave; "I will go with you. But I have something to do first. You go on around the hill *that* way, and I will hasten around *this* way, and meet you a little later near the grave."

So the six little boys went on as bidden until they came to a place near the grave. There they halted.

"Where is Brave?" they asked.

Now Brave, full of mischief, had thought to play a jest on his little friends. As soon as they were well out of sight he had sped around the hill to the shore of the lake and sticking his hands in the mud had rubbed it over his face, plastered it in his hair, and soiled his hands until he looked like a new risen corpse with the flesh rotting from his bones. He then went and lay down in the grave and awaited the boys.

When the six little boys came they were more timid than ever when they did not find Brave; but they feared to go back to the village without seeing the grave, for fear the old men would call them cowards.

So they slowly approached the grave and one of them timidly called out:

"Please, grandmother, we won't disturb your grave. We only want to see where you lie. Don't be angry."

At once a thin quavering voice, like an old woman's, called out:

"Han, han, takoja, hechetuya, hechetuya! Yes, yes, that's right, that's right."

The boys were frightened out of their senses, believing the old woman had come to life.

"Oh, grandmother," they gasped, "don't hurt us; please don't, we'll go."

Just then Brave raised his muddy face and hands up thru the choke cherry bushes. With the oozy mud dripping from his features he looked like some very witch just raised from the grave. The boys screamed outright. One fainted. The rest ran yelling up the hill to the village, where each broke at once for his mother's tepee.

As all the tents in a Dakota camping circle face the center, the boys as they came tearing into camp were in plain view from the tepees. Hearing the screaming, every woman in camp ran to her tepee door to see what had happened. Just then little Brave, as badly scared as the rest, came rushing in after them, his hair on end and covered with mud and crying out, all forgetful of his appearance:

"It's me, it's me!"

The women yelped and bolted in terror from the village. Brave dashed into his mother's tepee, scaring her out of her wits. Dropping pots and kettles, she tumbled out of the tent to run screaming with the rest. Nor would a single villager come near poor little Brave until he had gone down to the lake and washed himself.

The Bound Children

There once lived a widow with two children—the elder a daughter and the younger a son. The widow went in mourning for her husband a long time. She cut off her hair, let her dress lie untidy on her body and kept her face unpainted and unwashed.

There lived in the same village a great chief. He had one son just come old enough to marry. The chief had it known that he wished his son to take a wife, and all of the young women in the village were eager to marry the young man. However, he was pleased with none of them.

Now the widow thought, "I am tired of mourning for my husband and caring for my children. Perhaps if I lay aside my mourning and paint myself red, the chief's son may marry me."

So she slipped away from her two children, stole down to the river and made a bathing place thru the ice. When she had washed away all signs of mourning, she painted and decked herself and went to the chief's tepee. When his son saw her, he loved her, and a feast was made in honor of her wedding.

When the widow's daughter found herself forsaken, she wept bitterly. After a day or two she took her little brother in her arms and went to the tepee of an old woman who lived at one end of the village. The old woman's tumble down tepee was of bark and her dress and clothing was of old smoke-dried tent cover. But she was kind to the two waifs and took them in willingly.

The little girl was eager to find her mother. The old woman said to her: "I suspect your mother has painted her face red. Do not try to find her. If the chief's son marries her she will not want to be burdened with you."

The old woman was right. The girl went down to the river, and sure enough found a hole cut in the ice and about it lay the filth that the mother had washed from her body. The girl gathered up the filth and went on. By and by she came to a second hole in the ice. Here too was filth, but not so much as at the previous place. At the third hole the ice was clean.

The girl knew now that her mother had painted her face red. She went at once to the chief's tepee, raised the door flap and went in. There sat her mother with the chief's son at their wedding feast.

The girl walked up to her mother and hurled the filth in her mother's face.

"There," she cried, "you who forsake your helpless children and forget your husband, take that!"

And at once her mother became a hideous old woman.

The girl then went back to the lodge of the old woman, leaving the camp in an uproar. The chief soon sent some young warriors to seize the girl and her brother, and they were brought to his tent. He was furious with anger.

"Let the children be bound with lariats wrapped about their bodies and let them be left to starve. Our camp will move on," he said. The chief's son did not put away his wife, hoping she might be cured in some way and grow young again.

Everybody in camp now got ready to move; but the old woman came close to the girl and said:

"In my old tepee I have dug a hole and buried a pot with punk and steel and flint and packs of dried meat. They will tie you up like a corpse. But before we go I will come with a knife and pretend to stab you, but I will really cut the rope that binds you so that you can unwind it from your body as soon as the camp is out of sight and hearing."

And so, before the camp started, the old woman came to the place where the two children were bound. She had in her hand a knife bound to the end of a stick which she used as a lance. She stood over the children and cried aloud:

"You wicked girl, who have shamed your own mother, you deserve all the punishment that is given you. But after all I do not want to let you lie and starve. Far better kill you at once and have done with it!" and with her stick she stabbed many times, as if to kill, but she was really cutting the rope.

The camp moved on; but the children lay on the ground until noon the next day. Then they began to squirm about. Soon the girl was free, and she then set loose her little brother. They went at once to the old woman's hut where they found the flint and steel and the packs of dried meat.

The girl made her brother a bow and arrows and with these he killed birds and other small game.

The boy grew up a great hunter. They became rich. They built three great tepees, in one of which were stored rows upon rows of parfleche bags of dried meat.

One day as the brother went out to hunt, he met a handsome young stranger who greeted him and said to him:

"I know you are a good hunter, for I have been watching you; your sister, too, is industrious. Let me have her for a wife. Then you and I will be brothers and hunt together."

The girl's brother went home and told her what the young stranger had said.

"Brother, I do not care to marry," she answered. "I am now happy with you."

"But you will be yet happier married," he answered, "and the young stranger is of no mean family, as one can see by his dress and manners."

"Very well, I will do as you wish," she said. So the stranger came into the tepee and was the girl's husband.

One day as they were in their tent, a crow flew overhead, calling out loudly,

"*Kaw, Kaw,*

"They who forsook the children have no meat."

The girl and her husband and brother looked up at one another.

"What can it mean?" they asked. "Let us send for Unktomi (the spider). He is a good judge and he will know."

"And I will get ready a good dinner for him, for Unktomi is always hungry," added the young wife.

When Unktomi came, his yellow mouth opened with delight at the fine feast spread for him. After he had eaten he was told what the crow had said.

"The crow means," said Unktomi, "that the villagers and chief who bound and deserted you are in sad plight. They have hardly anything to eat and are starving."

When the girl heard this she made a bundle of choicest meat and called the crow.

"Take this to the starving villagers," she bade him.

He took the bundle in his beak, flew away to the starving village and dropped the bundle before the chief's tepee. The chief came out and the crow called loudly:

"Kaw, Kaw!

"The children who were forsaken have much meat; those who forsook them have none."

"What can he mean," cried the astonished villagers.

"Let us send for Unktomi," said one, "he is a great judge; he will tell us."

They divided the bundle of meat among the starving people, saving the biggest piece for Unktomi.

When Unktomi had come and eaten, the villagers told him of the crow and asked what the bird's words meant.

"He means," said Unktomi, "that the two children whom you forsook have tepees full of dried meat enough for all the village."

The villagers were filled with astonishment at this news. To find whether or not it was true, the chief called seven young men and sent them out to see. They came to the three tepees and there met the girl's brother and husband just going out to hunt (which they did now only for sport).

The girl's brother invited the seven young men into the third or sacred lodge, and after they had smoked a pipe and knocked out the ashes on a buffalo bone the brother gave them meat to eat, which the seven devoured greedily. The next day he loaded all seven with packs of meat, saying:

"Take this meat to the villagers and lead them hither."

While they awaited the return of the young men with the villagers, the girl made two bundles of meat, one of the best and choicest pieces, and the other of liver, very dry and hard to eat. After a few days the camp arrived. The young woman's mother opened the door and ran in crying: "Oh, my dear daughter, how glad I am to see you." But the daughter received her coldly and gave her the bundle of dried liver to eat. But when the old woman who had saved the children's lives came in, the young girl received her gladly, called her grandmother, and gave her the package of choice meat with marrow.

Then the whole village camped and ate of the stores of meat all the winter until spring came; and withal they were so many, there was such abundance of stores that there was still much left.

The Signs of Corn

When corn is to be planted by the Indians, it is the work of the women folk to see to the sorting and cleaning of the best seed. It is also the women's work to see to the planting. (This was in olden times.)

After the best seed has been selected, the planter measures the corn, lays down a layer of hay, then a layer of corn. Over this corn they sprinkle warm water and cover it with another layer of hay, then bind hay about the bundle and hang it up in a spot where the warm rays of the sun can strike it.

While the corn is hanging in the sun, the ground is being prepared to receive it. Having finished the task of preparing the ground, the woman takes down her seed corn which has by this time sprouted. Then she proceeds to plant the corn.

Before she plants the first hill, she extends her hoe heavenwards and asks the Great Spirit to bless her work, that she may have a good yield. After her prayer she takes four kernels and plants one at the north, one at the south, one at the east and one at the west sides of the first hill. This is asking the Great Spirit to give summer rain and sunshine to bring forth a good crop.

For different growths of the corn, the women have an interpretation as to the character of the one who planted it.

1st. Where the corn grows in straight rows and the cob is full of kernels to the end, this signifies that the planter of this corn is of an exemplary character, and is very truthful and thoughtful.

2nd. If the rows on the ears of corn are irregular and broken, the planter is considered careless and unthoughtful. Also disorderly and slovenly about her house and person.

3rd. When an ear of corn bears a few scattering kernels with spaces producing no corn, it is said that is a good sign that the planter will live to a ripe old age. So old will they be that like the corn, their teeth will be few and far between.

4th. When a stalk bears a great many nubbins, or small ears growing around the large one, it is a sign that the planter is from a large and respectable family.

After the corn is gathered, it is boiled into sweet corn and made into hominy; parched and mixed with buffalo tallow and rolled into round balls, and used at feasts, or carried by the warriors on the warpath as food.

When there has been a good crop of corn, an ear is always tied at the top of the medicine pole, of the sun dance, in thanks to the Great Spirit for his goodness to them in sending a bountiful crop.

Story of the Rabbits

The Rabbit nation were very much depressed in spirits on account of being run over by all other nations. They, being very obedient to their chief, obeyed all his orders to the letter. One of his orders was, that upon the approach of any other nation that they should follow the example of their chief and run up among the rocks and down into their burrows, and not show themselves until the strangers had passed.

This they always did. Even the chirp of a little cricket would send them all scampering to their dens.

One day they held a great council, and after talking over everything for some time, finally left it to their medicine man to decide. The medicine man arose and said:

"My friends, we are of no use on this earth. There isn't a nation on earth that fears us, and we are so timid that we cannot defend ourselves, so the best thing for us to do is to rid the earth of our nation, by all going over to the big lake and drowning ourselves."

This they decided to do; so going to the lake they were about to jump in, when they heard a splashing in the water. Looking, they saw a lot of frogs jumping into the lake.

"We will not drown ourselves," said the medicine man, "we have found a nation who are afraid of us. It is the frog nation." Had it not been for the frogs we would have had no rabbits, as the whole nation would have drowned themselves and the rabbit race would have been extinct.

How the Rabbit Lost his Tail

Once upon a time there were two brothers, one a great Genie and the other a rabbit. Like all genie, the older could change himself into any kind of an animal, bird, fish, cloud, thunder and lightning, or in fact anything that he desired.

The younger brother (the rabbit) was very mischievous and was continually getting into all kinds of trouble. His older brother was kept busy getting Rabbit out of all kinds of scrapes.

When Rabbit had attained his full growth he wanted to travel around and see something of the world. When he told his brother what he intended to do, the brother said: "Now, Rabbit, you are Witkotko (mischievous), so be very careful, and keep out of trouble as much as possible. In case you get into any serious trouble, and can't get out by yourself, just call on me for assistance, and no matter where you are, I will come to you."

Rabbit started out and the first day he came to a very high house, outside of which stood a very high pine tree. So high was the tree that Rabbit could hardly see the top. Outside the door, on an enormous stool, sat a very large giant fast asleep. Rabbit (having his bow and arrows with him) strung up his bow, and, taking an arrow from his quiver, said:

"I want to see how big this man is, so I guess I will wake him up." So saying he moved over to one side and took good aim, and shot the giant upon the nose. This stung like fire and awoke the giant, who jumped up, crying: "Who had the audacity to shoot me on the nose?" "I did," said Rabbit.

The giant, hearing a voice, looked all around, but saw nothing, until he looked down at the corner of the house, and there sat a rabbit.

"I had hiccoughs this morning and thought that I was going to have a good big meal, and here is nothing but a toothful."

"I guess you won't make a toothful of me," said Rabbit, "I am as strong as you, though I am little." "We will see," said the giant. He went into the house and came out, bringing a hammer that weighed many tons.

"Now, Mr. Rabbit, we will see who can throw this hammer over the top of that tree." "Get something harder to do," said Rabbit.

"Well, we will try this first," said the giant. With that he grasped the hammer in both hands, swung it three times around his head and sent it spinning thru the air. Up, up, it went, skimming the top of the tree, and came down, shaking the ground and burying itself deep into the earth.

"Now," said the giant, "if you don't accomplish this same feat, I am going to swallow you at one mouthful." Rabbit said, "I always sing to my brother before I attempt things like this." So he commenced singing and calling his brother. "Cinye! Cinye!" (brother, brother) he sang. The giant grew nervous, and said: "Boy, why do you call your brother?"

Pointing to a small black cloud that was approaching very swiftly, Rabbit said: "That is my brother; he can destroy you, your house, and pine tree in one breath."

"Stop him and you can go free," said the giant. Rabbit waved his paws and the cloud disappeared.

From this place Rabbit continued on his trip towards the west. The next day, while passing thru a deep forest, he thought he heard some one moaning, as though in pain. He stopped and listened; soon the wind blew and the moaning grew louder. Following the direction from whence came the sound, he soon discovered a man stripped of his clothing, and caught between two limbs of a tall elm tree. When the wind blew the limbs would rub together and squeeze the man, who would give forth the mournful groans.

"My, you have a fine place up there. Let us change. You can come down and I will take your place." (Now this man had been placed up there for punishment, by Rabbit's brother, and he could not get down unless some one came along and proposed to take his place on the tree). "Very well," said the man. "Take off your clothes and come up. I will fasten you in the limbs and you can have all the fun you want."

Rabbit disrobed and climbed up. The man placed him between the limbs and slid down the tree. He hurriedly got into Rabbit's clothes, and just as he had completed his toilet, the wind blew very hard. Rabbit was nearly crazy with pain, and screamed and cried. Then he began to cry "Cinye, Cinye" (brother, brother). "Call your brother as much as you like, he can never find me." So saying the man disappeared in the forest.

Scarcely had he disappeared, when the brother arrived, and seeing Rabbit in the tree, said: "Which way did he go?" Rabbit pointed the direction taken by the man. The brother flew over the top of the trees, soon found the man and brought him back, making him take his old place between the limbs, and causing a heavy wind to blow and continue all afternoon and night, for punishment to the man for having placed his brother up there.

After Rabbit got his clothes back on, his brother gave him a good scolding, and wound up by saying: "I want you to be more careful in the future. I have plenty of work to keep me as busy as I want to be, and I can't be stopping every little while to be making trips to get you out of some foolish scrape. It was only yesterday that I came five hundred miles to help you from the giant, and today I have had to come a thousand miles, so be more careful from this on."

Several days after this the Rabbit was traveling along the banks of a small river, when he came to a small clearing in the woods, and in the center of the clearing stood a nice little log hut. Rabbit was wondering who could be living here when the door slowly opened and an old man appeared in the doorway, bearing a tripe water pail in his right hand. In his left hand he held a string which was fastened to the inside of the house. He kept hold of the string and came slowly down to the river. When he got to the water he stooped down and dipped the pail into it and returned to the house, still holding the string for guidance.

Soon he reappeared holding on to another string, and, following this one, went to a large pile of wood and returned to the house with it. Rabbit wanted to see if the old man would come out again, but he came out no more. Seeing smoke ascending from the mud chimney, he thought he would go over and see what the old man was doing. He knocked at the door, and a weak voice bade him enter. He noticed that the old man was cooking dinner.

"Hello Tunkasina (grandfather), you must have a nice time, living here alone. I see that you have everything handy. You can get wood and water, and that is all you have to do. How do you get your provisions?"

"The wolves bring my meat, the mice my rice and ground beans, and the birds bring me the cherry leaves for my tea. Yet it is a hard life, as I am all alone most of the time and have no one to talk to, and besides, I am blind."

"Say, grandfather," said Rabbit, "let us change places. I think I would like to live here."

"If we exchange clothes," said the other, "you will become old and blind, while I will assume your youth and good looks." (Now, this old man was placed here for punishment by Rabbit's brother. He had killed his wife, so the genie made him old and blind, and he would remain so until some one came who would exchange places with him).

"I don't care for youth and good looks," said Rabbit, "let us make the change."

They changed clothes, and Rabbit became old and blind, whilst the old man became young and handsome.

"Well, I must go," said the man. He went out and cutting the strings close to the door, ran off laughing. "You will get enough of your living alone, you crazy boy," and saying this he ran into the woods.

Rabbit thought he would like to get some fresh water and try the string paths so that he would get accustomed to it. He bumped around the room and finally found the tripe water bucket. He took hold of the string and started out. When he had gotten a short distance from the door he came to the end of the string so suddenly, that he lost the end which he had in his hand, and he wandered about, bumping against the trees, and tangling himself up in plum bushes and thorns, scratching his face and hands so badly that the blood ran from them. Then it was that he commenced again to cry, "Cinye! Cinye!" (brother, brother). Soon his brother arrived, and asked which way the old man had gone.

"I don't know," said Rabbit, "I couldn't see which path he took, as I was blind."

The genie called the birds, and they came flying from every direction. As fast as they arrived the brother asked them if they had seen the man whom he had placed here for punishment, but none had seen him. The owl came last, and when asked if he had seen the man, he said "hoo-hoo." "The man who lived here," said the brother. "Last night I was hunting mice in the woods south of here and I saw a man sleeping beneath a plum tree. I thought it was your brother, Rabbit, so I didn't awaken him," said the owl.

"Good for you, owl," said the brother, "for this good news, you shall hereafter roam around only at night, and I will fix your eyes, so the darker the night the better you will be able to see. You will always have the fine cool nights to hunt your food. You other birds can hunt your food during the hot daylight." (Since then the owl has been the night bird).

The brother flew to the woods and brought the man back and cut the strings short, and said to him: "Now you can get a taste of what you gave my brother."

To Rabbit he said: "I ought not to have helped you this time. Any one who is so crazy as to change places with a blind man should be left without help, so be careful, as I am getting tired of your foolishness, and will not help you again if you do anything as foolish as you did this time."

Rabbit started to return to his home. When he had nearly completed his journey he came to a little creek, and being thirsty took a good long drink. While he was drinking he heard a noise as though a wolf or cat was scratching the earth. Looking up to a hill which overhung the creek, he saw four wolves, with their tails intertwined, pulling with all their might. As Rabbit came up to them one pulled loose, and Rabbit saw that his tail was broken.

"Let me pull tails with you. My tail is long and strong," said Rabbit, and the wolves assenting, Rabbit interlocked his long tail with those of the three wolves and commenced pulling and the wolves pulled so hard that they pulled Rabbit's tail off at the second joint. The wolves disappeared.

"Cinye! Cinye! (Brother, brother.) I have lost my tail," cried Rabbit. The genie came and seeing his brother Rabbit's tail missing, said: "You look better without a tail anyway."

From that time on rabbits have had no tails.

UNKTOMI AND THE ARROWHEADS

There were once upon a time two young men who were very great friends, and were constantly together. One was a very thoughtful young man, the other very impulsive, who never stopped to think before he committed an act.

One day these two friends were walking along, telling each other of their experiences in love making. They ascended a high hill, and on reaching the top, heard a ticking noise as if small stones or pebbles were being struck together.

Looking around they discovered a large spider sitting in the midst of a great many flint arrowheads. The spider was busily engaged making the flint rocks into arrow heads. They looked at the spider, but he never moved, but continued hammering away on a piece of flint which he had nearly completed into another arrowhead.

"Let's hit him," said the thoughtless one. "No," said the other, "he is not harming any one; in fact, he is doing a great good, as he is making the flint arrowheads which we use to point our arrows."

"Oh, you are afraid," said the first young man. "He can't harm you, just watch me hit him." So saying, he picked up an arrowhead and throwing it at "Unktomi," hit him on the side. As Unktomi rolled over on his side, got up and stood looking at them, the young man laughed and said: "Well, let us be going, as your grandfather, "Unktomi," doesn't seem to like our company." They started down the hill, when suddenly the one who had hit Unktomi took a severe fit of coughing. He coughed and coughed, and finally small particles of blood came from his mouth. The blood kept coming thicker and in great gushes. Finally it came so thick and fast that the man could not get his breath and fell upon the ground dead.

The thoughtful young man, seeing that his friend was no more, hurried to the village and reported what had happened. The relatives and friends hurried to the hill, and sure enough, there lay the thoughtless young man still and cold in death. They held a council and sent for the chief of the Unktomi tribe. When he heard what had happened, he told the council that he could do nothing to his Unktomi, as it had only defended itself.

Said he: "My friends, seeing that your tribe was running short of arrowheads, I set a great many of my tribe to work making flint arrowheads for you. When my men are thus engaged they do not wish to be disturbed, and your young man not only disturbed my man, but grossly insulted him by striking him with one of the arrowheads which he had worked so hard to make. My man could not sit and take this insult, so as the young man walked away the Unktomi shot him with a very tiny arrowhead. This produced a hemorrhage, which caused his death. So now, my friends, if you will fill and pass the peace pipe, we will part good friends and my tribe shall always furnish you with plenty of flint arrowheads." So saying, Unktomi Tanka finished his peace smoke and returned to his tribe.

Ever after that, when the Indians heard a ticking in the grass, they would go out of their way to get around the sound, saying, Unktomi is making arrowheads; we must not disturb him.

Thus it was that Unktomi Tanka (Big Spider) had the respect of this tribe, and was never after disturbed in his work of making arrowheads.

The Bear and the Rabbit Hunt Buffalo

O nce upon a time there lived as neighbors, a bear and a rabbit. The rabbit was a good shot, and the bear being very clumsy could not use the arrow to good advantage. The bear was very unkind to the rabbit. Every morning, the bear would call over to the rabbit and say: "Take your bow and arrows and come with me to the other side of the hill. A large herd of buffalo are grazing there, and I want you to shoot some of them for me, as my children are crying for meat."

The rabbit, fearing to arouse the bear's anger by refusing, consented, and went with the bear, and shot enough buffalo to satisfy the hungry family. Indeed, he shot and killed so many that there was lots of meat left after the bear and his family had loaded themselves, and packed all they could carry home. The bear being very gluttonous, and not wanting the rabbit to get any of the meat, said: "Rabbit, you come along home with us and we will return and get the remainder of the meat."

The poor rabbit could not even taste the blood from the butchering, as the bear would throw earth on the blood and dry it up. Poor Rabbit would have to go home hungry after his hard day's work.

The bear was the father of five children. The youngest boy was very kind to the rabbit. The mother bear, knowing that her youngest was a very hearty eater, always gave him an extra large piece of meat. What the baby bear did not eat, he would take outside with him and pretend to play ball with it, kicking it toward the rabbit's house, and when he got close to the door he would give the meat such a great kick, that it would fly into the rabbit's house, and in this way poor Rabbit would get his meal unknown to the papa bear.

Baby bear never forgot his friend Rabbit. Papa bear often wondered why his baby would go outside after each meal. He grew suspicious and asked the baby where he had been. "Oh, I always play ball outside, around the house, and when I get tired playing I eat up my meat ball and then come in."

The baby bear was too cunning to let papa bear know that he was keeping his friend rabbit from starving to death. Nevertheless, papa bear suspected baby and said: "Baby, I think you go over to the rabbit's after every meal."

The four older brothers were very handsome, but baby bear was a little puny fellow, whose coat couldn't keep out much cold, as it was short and shaggy, and of a dirty brown color. The three older brothers were very unkind to baby bear, but the fourth one always took baby's part, and was always kind to his baby brother.

Rabbit was getting tired of being ordered and bullied around by papa bear. He puzzled his brain to scheme some way of getting even with Mr. Bear for abusing him so much. He studied all night long, but no scheme worth trying presented itself. Early one morning Mr. Bear presented himself at Rabbit's door.

"Say, Rabbit, my meat is all used up, and there is a fine herd of buffalo grazing on the hillside. Get your bow and arrows and come with me. I want you to shoot some of them for me."

"Very well," said Rabbit, and he went and killed six buffalo for Bear. Bear got busy butchering and poor Rabbit, thinking he would get a chance to lick up one mouthful of blood, stayed very close to the bear while he was cutting up the meat. The bear was very watchful lest the rabbit get something to eat. Despite bear's watchfulness, a small clot of blood rolled past and behind the bear's feet. At once Rabbit seized the clot and hid it in his bosom. By the time Rabbit got home, the blood clot was hardened from the warmth of his body, so, being hungry, it put Mr. Rabbit out of sorts to think that after all his trouble he could not eat the blood.

Very badly disappointed, he lay down on his floor and gazed up into the chimney hole. Disgusted with the way things had turned out, he grabbed up the blood clot and threw it up through the hole. Scarcely had it hit the ground when he heard the voice of a baby crying, "Ate! Ate!" (father, father). He went outside and there he found a big baby boy. He took the baby into his house and threw him out through the hole again. This time the boy was large enough to say "Ate, Ate, he-cun-sin-lo." (Father, father, don't do that). But nevertheless, he threw him up and out again. On going out the third time, there stood a handsome youth smiling at him. Rabbit at once adopted the youth and took him into his house, seating him in the seat of honor (which is directly opposite the entrance), and saying: "My son, I want you to be a good, honest, straightforward man. Now, I have in my possession a fine outfit, and you, my son, shall wear it."

Suiting his action to his words, he drew out a bag from a hollow tree and on opening it, drew out a fine buckskin shirt (tanned white as snow), worked with porcupine quills. Also a pair of red leggings worked with beads. Moccasins worked with colored hair. A fine otter skin robe. White weasel skins to intertwine with his beautiful long black locks. A magnificent center eagle feather. A rawhide covered bow, accompanied by a quiver full of flint arrowheads.

The rabbit, having dressed his son in all the latest finery, sat back and gazed long and lovingly at his handsome son. Instinctively Rabbit felt that his son had been sent him for the purpose of being instrumental in the downfall of Mr. Bear. Events will show.

The morning following the arrival of Rabbit's son, Mr. Bear again presents himself at the door, crying out: "You lazy, ugly rabbit, get up and come out here. I want you to shoot some more buffalo for me."

"Who is this, who speaks so insultingly to you, father?" asked the son.

"It is a bear who lives near here, and makes me kill buffalo for his family, and he won't let me take even one little drop of blood from the killing, and consequently, my son, I have nothing in my house for you to eat."

The young man was anxious to meet Mr. Bear but Rabbit advised him to wait a little until he and Bear had gone to the hunt. So the son obeyed, and when he thought it time that the killing was done, he started out and arrived on the scene just as Mr. Bear was about to proceed with his butchering.

Seeing a strange shadow on the ground beside him, Mr. Bear looked up and gazed into the fearless eyes of rabbit's handsome son.

"Who is this?" asked Mr. Bear of poor little Rabbit.

"I don't know," answered Rabbit.

"Who are you?" asked the bear of Rabbit's son. "Where did you come from?"

The rabbit's son not replying, the bear spoke thus to him: "Get out of here, and get out quick, too."

At this speech the rabbit's son became angered, and fastened an arrow to his bow and drove the arrow through the bear's heart. Then he turned on Mrs. Bear and served her likewise. During the melee, Rabbit shouted: "My son, my son, don't kill the two youngest. The baby has kept me from starving and the other one is good and kind to his baby brother."

So the three older brothers who were unkind to their baby brother met a similar fate to that of their selfish parents.

This (the story goes) is the reason that bears travel only in pairs.

The Brave Who Went on the Warpath
Alone and Won the Name of
the Lone Warrior

There was once a young man whose parents were not overburdened with the riches of this world, and consequently could not dress their only son in as rich a costume as the other young men of the tribe, and on account of not being so richly clad as they, he was looked down upon and shunned by them. He was never invited to take part in any of their sports; nor was he ever asked to join any of the war parties.

In the village lived an old man with an only daughter. Like the other family, they were poor, but the daughter was the belle of the tribe. She was the most sought after by the young men of the village, and warriors from tribes far distant came to press their suit at winning her for their bride. All to no purpose; she had the same answer for them as she had for the young men of the village.

The poor young man was also very handsome despite his poor clothes, but having never killed an enemy nor brought home any enemies' horses he was not (according to Indian rules) allowed to make love to any young or old woman. He tried in vain to join some of the war parties, that he might get the chance to win his spurs as a warrior. To all his pleadings, came the same answer: "You are not fit to join a war party. You have no horses, and if you should get killed our tribe would be laughed at and be made fun of as you have such poor clothes, and we don't want the enemy to know that we have any one of our tribe who dresses so poorly as you do."

Again, and again, he tried different parties, only to be made fun of and insulted.

One night he sat in the poor tepee of his parents. He was in deep study and had nothing to say. His father, noticing his melancholy mood, asked him what had happened to cause him to be so quiet, as he was always of a jolly disposition. The son answered and said:

"Father, I am going on the warpath alone. In vain I have tried to be a member of one of the war parties. To all of my pleadings I have got nothing but insults in return."

"But my son, you have no gun nor ammunition. Where can you get any and how can you get it? We have nothing to buy one for you with," said the father.

"I don't need any weapons. I am going to bring back some of the enemies' horses, and I don't need a gun for that."

Early the next morning (regardless of the old couple's pleadings not to go unarmed) the young man left the village and headed northwest, the direction always taken by the war parties.

For ten days he traveled without seeing any signs of a camp. The evening of the tenth day, he reached a very high butte, thickly wooded at the summit. He ascended this butte, and as he sat there between two large boulders, watching the beautiful rays of the setting sun, he was suddenly startled to hear the neigh of a horse. Looking down into the beautiful valley which was threaded by a beautiful creek fringed with timber, he noticed close to the base of the butte upon which he sat, a large drove of horses grazing peacefully and quietly. Looking closer, he noticed at a little distance from the main drove, a horse with a saddle on his back. This was the one that had neighed, as the drove drifted further away from him. He was tied by a long lariat to a large sage bush.

Where could the rider be, he said to himself. As if in answer to his question, there appeared not more than twenty paces from him a middle aged man coming up through a deep ravine. The man was evidently in search of some kind of game, as he held his gun in readiness for instant use, and kept his eyes directed at every crevice and clump of bush. So intent was he on locating the game he was trailing, that he never noticed the young man who sat like a statue not twenty paces away. Slowly and cautiously the man approached, and when he had advanced to within a few paces of the young man he stopped and turning around, stood looking down into the valley. This was the only chance that our brave young friend had. Being unarmed, he would stand no show if the enemy ever got a glimpse of him. Slowly and noiselessly he drew his hunting knife (which his father had given him on his departure from home) and holding it securely in his right hand, gathered himself and gave a leap which landed him upon the unsuspecting enemy's shoulders. The force with which he landed on the enemy caused him (the enemy) to lose his hold on his gun, and it went rattling down into the chasm, forty feet below.

Down they came together, the young man on top. No sooner had they struck the ground than the enemy had out his knife, and then commenced a hand to hand duel. The enemy, having more experience, was getting the best of our young friend. Already our young friend had two ugly cuts, one across his chest and the other through his forearm.

He was becoming weak from the loss of blood, and could not stand the killing pace much longer. Summoning all his strength for one more trial to overcome his antagonist, he rushed him toward the chasm, and in his hurry to get away from this fierce attack, the enemy stepped back one step too far, and down they both went into the chasm. Interlocked in each other's arms, the young man drove his knife into the enemy's side and when they struck the bottom the enemy relaxed his hold and straightened out stiff and dead.

Securing his scalp and gun, the young man proceeded down to where the horse was tied to the sage bush, and then gathering the drove of horses proceeded on his return to his own village. Being wounded severely he had to ride very slowly. All the long hours of the night he drove the horses towards his home village.

In the meantime, those at the enemies' camp wondered at the long absence of the herder who was watching their drove of horses, and finally seven young men went to search for the missing herder. All night long they searched the hillsides for the horses and herder, and when it had grown light enough in the morning they saw by the ground where there had been a fierce struggle.

Following the tracks in the sand and leaves, they came to the chasm where the combatants had fallen over, and there, lying on his back staring up at them in death, was their herder. They hastened to the camp and told what they had found. Immediately the warriors mounted their war ponies (these ponies are never turned loose, but kept tied close to the tepee of the owner), and striking the trail of the herd driven off by our young friend, they urged forth their ponies and were soon far from their camp on the trail of our young friend. All day long they traveled on his trail, and just as the sun was sinking they caught sight of him driving the drove ahead over a high hill. Again they urged forth their tired ponies. The young man, looking back along the trail, saw some dark objects coming along, and, catching a fresh horse, drove the rest ahead at a great rate. Again all night he drove them, and when daylight came he looked back (from a high butte) over his trail and saw coming over a distant raise, two horsemen. These two undoubtedly rode the best ponies, as he saw nothing of the others. Driving the horses into a thick belt of timber, he concealed himself close to the trail made by the drove of horses, and lay in ambush for the two daring horsemen who had followed him so far. Finally they appeared on the butte from where he had looked back and saw them following him. For a long time they

MARIE L. MCLAUGHLIN

sat there scouring the country before them in hopes that they might see some signs of their stolen horses. Nothing could they see. Had they but known, their horses were but a few hundred yards from them, but the thick timber securely hid them from view. Finally one of them arose and pointed to the timber. Then leaving his horse in charge of his friend, he descended the butte and followed the trail of the drove to where they had entered the timber. Little did he think that he was standing on the brink of eternity. The young man hiding not more than a hundred yards from him could have shot him there where he stood, but wanting to play fair, he stepped into sight. When he did, the enemy took quick aim and fired. He was too hasty. Had he taken more careful aim he might have killed our young friend, but his bullet whizzed harmlessly over the young man's head and buried itself in a tree. The young man took good aim and fired. The enemy threw up both hands and fell forward on his face. The other one on the hill, seeing his friend killed, hastily mounted his horse and leading his friend's horse, made rapidly off down the butte in the direction from whence he had come. Waiting for some time to be sure the one who was alive did not come up and take a shot at him, he finally advanced upon the fallen enemy and securing his gun, ammunition and scalp, went to his horse and drove the herd on through the woods and crossing a long flat prairie, ascended a long chain of hills and sat looking back along his trail in search of any of the enemy who might continue to follow him.

Thus he sat until the long shadows of the hills reminded him that it would soon be sunset, and as he must get some sleep, he wanted to find some creek bend where he could drive the bunch of ponies and feel safe as to their not straying off during the night. He found a good place for the herd, and catching a fresh horse, he picketed him close to where he was going to sleep, and wrapping himself in his blanket, was soon fast asleep. So tired and sleepy was he that a heavy rain which had come up, during the night, soaked him through and through, but he never awakened until the sun was high in the east.

He awoke and going to the place where he had left the herd, he was glad to find them all there. He mounted his horse and started his herd homeward again. For two days he drove them, and on the evening of the second day he came in sight of the village.

The older warriors, hearing of the young man going on this trip alone and unarmed, told the parents to go in mourning for their son, as he would never come back alive. When the people of the village saw this large drove of horses advancing towards them, they at first thought it was a war party of the enemy, and so the head men called the young warriors together and fully prepared for a great battle. They advanced upon the supposed enemy. When they got close enough to discern a lone horseman driving this large herd, they surrounded the horses and lone warrior, and brought him triumphantly into camp. On arriving in the camp (or village) the horses were counted and the number counted up to one hundred and ten head.

The chief and his criers (or heralds) announced through the whole village that there would be a great war dance given in honor of the Lone Warrior.

The whole village turned out and had a great war dance that was kept up three days and three nights. The two scalps which the young man had taken were tied to a pole which was placed in the center of the dance circle. At this dance, the Lone Warrior gave to each poor family five head of horses.

Being considered eligible now to pay his respects to any girl who took his fancy, he at once went to the camp of the beautiful girl of the tribe, and as he was always her choice, she at once consented to marry him.

The news spread through the village that Lone Warrior had won the belle of the nation for his bride, and this with the great feat which he had accomplished alone in killing two enemies and bringing home a great herd of horses, raised him to the rank of chief, which he faithfully filled to the end of his days. And many times he had to tell his grandchildren the story of how he got the name of the Lone Warrior.

THE SIOUX WHO MARRIED THE
CROW CHIEF'S DAUGHTER

A war party of seven young men, seeing a lone tepee standing on the edge of a heavy belt of timber, stopped and waited for darkness, in order to send one of their scouts ahead to ascertain whether the camp which they had seen was the camp of friend or enemy.

When darkness had settled down on them, and they felt secure in not being detected, they chose one of their scouts to go on alone and find out what would be the best direction for them to advance upon the camp, should it prove to be an enemy.

Among the scouts was one who was noted for his bravery, and many were the brave acts he had performed. His name was Big Eagle. This man they selected to go to the lone camp and obtain the information for which they were waiting.

Big Eagle was told to look carefully over the ground and select the best direction from which they should make the attack. The other six would await his return. He started on his mission, being careful not to make any noise. He stealthily approached the camp. As he drew near to the tent he was surprised to note the absence of any dogs, as these animals are always kept by the Sioux to notify the owners by their barking of the approach of anyone. He crawled up to the tepee door, and peeping through a small aperture, he saw three persons sitting inside. An elderly man and woman were sitting at the right of the fireplace, and a young woman at the seat of honor, opposite the door.

Big Eagle had been married and his wife had died five winters previous to the time of this episode. He had never thought of marrying again, but when he looked upon this young woman he thought he was looking upon the face of his dead wife. He removed his cartridge belts and knife, and placing them, along with his rifle, at the side of the tent, he at once boldly stepped inside the tepee, and going over to the man, extended his hand and shook first the man's hand, then the old woman's, and lastly the young woman's. Then he seated himself by the side of the girl, and thus they sat, no one speaking.

Finally, Big Eagle made signs to the man, explaining as well as possible by signs, that his wife had died long ago, and when he saw the girl she so strongly resembled his dead wife that he wished to marry her, and he would go back to the enemy's camp and live with them, if they would consent to the marriage of their daughter.

The old man seemed to understand, and Big Eagle again made signs to him that a party were lying in wait just a short distance from his camp. Noiselessly they brought in the horses, and taking down the tent, they at once moved off in the direction from whence they had come. The war party waited all night, and when the first rays of dawn disclosed to them the absence of the tepee, they at once concluded that Big Eagle had been discovered and killed, so they hurriedly started on their trail for home.

In the meantime, the hunting party, for this it was that Big Eagle had joined, made very good time in putting a good distance between themselves and the war party. All day they traveled, and when evening came they ascended a high hill, looking down into the valley on the other side. There stretched for two miles, along the banks of a small stream, an immense camp. The old man made signs for Big Eagle to remain with the two women where he was, until he could go to the camp and prepare them to receive an enemy into their village.

The old man rode through the camp and drew up at the largest tepee in the village. Soon Big Eagle could see men gathering around the tepee. The crowd grew larger and larger, until the whole village had assembled at the large tepee. Finally they dispersed, and catching their horses, mounted and advanced to the hill on which Big Eagle and the two women were waiting. They formed a circle around them and slowly they returned to the village, singing and riding in a circle around them.

When they arrived at the village they advanced to the large tepee, and motioned Big Eagle to the seat of honor in the tepee. In the village was a man who understood and spoke the Sioux language. He was sent for, and through him the oath of allegiance to the Crow tribe was taken by Big Eagle. This done he was presented with the girl to wife, and also with many spotted ponies.

Big Eagle lived with his wife among her people for two years, and during this time he joined in four different battles between his own people (the Sioux) and the Crow people, to whom his wife belonged.

In no battle with his own people would he carry any weapons, only a long willow coup-stick, with which he struck the fallen Sioux.

At the expiration of two years he concluded to pay a visit to his own tribe, and his father-in-law, being a chief of high standing, at once had it heralded through the village that his son-in-law would visit his own people, and for them to show their good will and respect for him by bringing ponies for his son-in-law to take back to his people.

Hearing this, the herds were all driven in and all day long horses were brought to the tent of Big Eagle, and when he was ready to start on his homeward trip, twenty young men were elected to accompany him to within a safe distance of his village. The twenty young men drove the gift horses, amounting to two hundred and twenty head, to within one day's journey of the village of Big Eagle, and fearing for their safety from his people, Big Eagle sent them back to their own village.

On his arrival at his home village, they received him as one returned from the dead, as they were sure he had been killed the night he had been sent to reconnoiter the lone camp. There was great feasting and dancing in honor of his return, and the horses were distributed among the needy ones of the village.

Remaining at his home village for a year, he one day made up his mind to return to his wife's people. A great many fancy robes, dresses, war bonnets, moccasins, and a great drove of horses were given him, and his wife, and he bade farewell to his people for good, saying, "I will never return to you again, as I have decided to live the remainder of my days with my wife's people."

On his arrival at the village of the Crows, he found his father-in-law at the point of death. A few days later the old man died, and Big Eagle was appointed to fill the vacancy of chief made by the death of his father-in-law.

Subsequently he took part in battles against his own people, and in the third battle was killed on the field. Tenderly the Crow warriors bore him back to their camp, and great was the mourning in the Crow village for the brave man who always went into battle unarmed, save only the willow wand which he carried.

Thus ended the career of one of the bravest of Sioux warriors who ever took the scalp of an enemy, and who for the love of his dead wife, gave up home, parents, and friends, to be killed on the field of battle by his own tribe.

The Boy and the Turtles

A boy went on a turtle hunt, and after following the different streams for hours, finally came to the conclusion that the only place he would find any turtles would be at the little lake, where the tribe always hunted them.

So, leaving the stream he had been following, he cut across country to the lake. On drawing near the lake he crawled on his hands and knees in order not to be seen by the turtles, who were very watchful, as they had been hunted so much. Peeping over the rock he saw a great many out on the shore sunning themselves, so he very cautiously undressed, so he could leap into the water and catch them before they secreted themselves. But on pulling off his shirt one of his hands was held up so high that the turtles saw it and jumped into the lake with a great splash.

The boy ran to the shore, but saw only bubbles coming up from the bottom. Directly the boy saw something coming to the surface, and soon it came up into sight. It was a little man, and soon others, by the hundreds, came up and swam about, splashing the water up into the air to a great height. So scared was the boy that he never stopped to gather up his clothes but ran home naked and fell into his grandmother's tent door.

"What is the trouble, grandchild," cried the old woman. But the boy could not answer. "Did you see anything unnatural?" He shook his head, "no." He made signs to the grandmother that his lungs were pressing so hard against his sides that he could not talk. He kept beating his side with his clenched hands. The grandmother got out her medicine bag, made a prayer to the Great Spirit to drive out the evil spirit that had entered her grandson's body, and after she had applied the medicine, the prayer must have been heard and answered, as the boy commenced telling her what he had heard and seen.

The grandmother went to the chief's tent and told what her grandson had seen. The chief sent two brave warriors to the lake to ascertain whether it was true or not. The two warriors crept to the little hill close to the lake, and there, sure enough, the lake was swarming with little men swimming about, splashing the water high up into the air. The warriors, too, were scared and hurried home, and in the council called on their return told what they had seen. The boy was brought to the council and given the seat of honor (opposite the door), and was named "Wankan Wanyanka" (sees holy).

The lake had formerly borne the name of Truth Lake, but from this time on was called "Wicasa-bde"—Man Lake.

The Hermit, or the Gift of Corn

In a deep forest, far from the villages of his people, lived a hermit. His tent was made of buffalo skins, and his dress was made of deer skin. Far from the haunts of any human being this old hermit was content to spend his days.

All day long he would wander through the forest studying the different plants of nature and collecting precious roots, which he used as medicine. At long intervals some warrior would arrive at the tent of the old hermit and get medicine roots from him for the tribe, the old hermit's medicine being considered far superior to all others.

After a long day's ramble in the woods, the hermit came home late, and being very tired, at once lay down on his bed and was just dozing off to sleep, when he felt something rub against his foot. Awakening with a start, he noticed a dark object and an arm was extended to him, holding in its hand a flint pointed arrow.

The hermit thought, "This must be a spirit, as there is no human being around here but myself!" A voice then said: "Hermit, I have come to invite you to my home." "How (yes), I will come," said the old hermit. Wherewith he arose, wrapped his robe about him and followed.

Outside the door he stopped and looked around, but could see no signs of the dark object.

"Whoever you are, or whatever you be, wait for me, as I don't know where to go to find your house," said the hermit. Not an answer did he receive, nor could he hear any noises as though anyone was walking through the brush. Re-entering his tent he retired and was soon fast asleep. The next night the same thing occurred again, and the hermit followed the object out, only to be left as before.

He was very angry to think that anyone should be trying to make sport of him, and he determined to find out who this could be who was disturbing his night's rest.

The next evening he cut a hole in the tent large enough to stick an arrow through, and stood by the door watching. Soon the dark object came and stopped outside of the door, and said: "Grandfather, I came to—," but he never finished the sentence, for the old man let go his arrow, and he heard the arrow strike something which produced a sound as though he had shot into a sack of pebbles. He did not go out that night to see what his arrow had struck, but early next morning he went out and looked at the spot about where he thought the object had stood. There on the ground lay a little heap of corn, and from this little heap a small line of corn lay scattered along a path. This he followed far into the woods. When he came to a very small knoll the trail ended. At the end of the trail was a large circle, from which the grass had been scraped off clean.

"The corn trail stops at the edge of this circle," said the old man, "so this must be the home of whoever it was that invited me." He took his bone knife and hatchet and proceeded to dig down into the center of the circle. When he had got down to the length of his arm, he came to a sack of dried meat. Next he found a sack of Indian turnips, then a sack of dried cherries; then a sack of corn, and last of all another sack, empty except that there was about a cupful of corn in one corner of it, and that the sack had a hole in the other corner where his arrow had pierced it. From this hole in the sack the corn was scattered along the trail, which guided the old man to the cache.*

From this the hermit taught the tribes how to keep their provisions when traveling and were overloaded. He explained to them how they should dig a pit and put their provisions into it and cover them with earth. By this method the Indians used to keep provisions all summer, and when fall came they would return to their cache, and on opening it would find everything as fresh as the day they were placed there.

The old hermit was also thanked as the discoverer of corn, which had never been known to the Indians until discovered by the old hermit.

---

*Hiding place.

THE MYSTERIOUS BUTTE

A young man was once hunting and came to a steep hill. The east side of the hill suddenly dropped off to a very steep bank. He stood on this bank, and at the base he noticed a small opening. On going down to examine it more closely, he found it was large enough to admit a horse or buffalo. On either side of the door were figures of different animals engraved into the wall.

He entered the opening and there, scattered about on the floor, lay many bracelets, pipes and many other things of ornament, as though they had been offerings to some great spirit. He passed through this first room and on entering the second it was so dark that he could not see his hands before his face, so becoming scared, he hurriedly left the place, and returning home told what he had seen.

Upon hearing this the chief selected four of his most daring warriors to go with this young man and investigate and ascertain whether the young man was telling the truth or not. The five proceeded to the butte, and at the entrance the young man refused to go inside, as the figures on either side of the entrance had been changed.

The four entered and seeing that all in the first chamber was as the young man had told, they went on to the next chamber and found it so dark that they could not see anything. They continued on, however, feeling their way along the walls. They finally found an entrance that was so narrow that they had to squeeze into it sideways. They felt their way around the walls and found another entrance, so low down that they had to crawl on their hands and knees to go through into the next chamber.

On entering the last chamber they found a very sweet odor coming from the opposite direction. Feeling around and crawling on their hands and knees, they discovered a hole in the floor leading downward. From this hole came up the sweet odor. They hurriedly held a council, and decided to go no further, but return to the camp and report what they had found. On getting to the first chamber one of the young men said: "I am going to take these bracelets to show that we are telling the truth." "No," said the other three, "this being the abode of some Great Spirit, you may have some accident befall you for taking what is not yours." "Ah! You fellows are like old women," said he, taking a fine bracelet and encircling his left wrist with it.

When they reached the village they reported what they had seen. The young man exhibited the bracelet to prove that it was the truth they had told.

Shortly after this, these four young men were out fixing up traps for wolves. They would raise one end of a heavy log and place a stick under, bracing up the log. A large piece of meat was placed about five feet away from the log and this space covered with poles and willows. At the place where the upright stick was put, a hole was left open, large enough to admit the body of a wolf. The wolf, scenting the meat and unable to get at it through the poles and willows, would crowd into the hole and working his body forward, in order to get the meat, would push down the brace and the log thus released would hold the wolf fast under its weight.

The young man with the bracelet was placing his bait under the log when he released the log by knocking down the brace, and the log caught his wrist on which he wore the bracelet. He could not release himself and called loud and long for assistance. His friends, hearing his call, came to his assistance, and on lifting the log found the young man's wrist broken. "Now," said they, "you have been punished for taking the wristlet out of the chamber of the mysterious butte."

Some time after this a young man went to the butte and saw engraved on the wall a woman holding in her hand a pole, with which she was holding up a large amount of beef which had been laid across another pole, which had broken in two from the weight of so much meat.

He returned to the camp and reported what he had seen. All around the figure he saw marks of buffalo hoofs, also marked upon the wall.

The next day an enormous herd of buffalo came near to the village, and a great many were killed. The women were busy cutting up and drying the meat. At one camp was more meat than at any other. The woman was hanging meat upon a long tent pole, when the pole broke in two and she was obliged to hold the meat up with another pole, just as the young man saw on the mysterious butte.

Ever after that the Indians paid weekly visits to this butte, and thereon would read the signs that were to govern their plans.

This butte was always considered the prophet of the tribe.

THE WONDERFUL TURTLE

Near to a Chippewa village lay a large lake, and in this lake there lived an enormous turtle. This was no ordinary turtle, as he would often come out of his home in the lake and visit with his Indian neighbors. He paid the most of his visits to the head chief, and on these occasions would stay for hours, smoking and talking with him.

The chief, seeing that the turtle was very smart and showed great wisdom in his talk, took a great fancy to him, and whenever any puzzling subject came up before the chief, he generally sent for Mr. Turtle to help him decide.

One day there came a great misunderstanding between different parties of the tribe, and so excited became both sides that it threatened to cause bloodshed. The chief was unable to decide for either faction, so he said, "I will call Mr. Turtle. He will judge for you."

Sending for the turtle, the chief vacated his seat for the time being, until the turtle should hear both sides, and decide which was in the right. The turtle came, and taking the chief's seat, listened very attentively to both sides, and thought long before he gave his decision. After thinking long and studying each side carefully, he came to the conclusion to decide in favor of both. This would not cause any hard feelings. So he gave them a lengthy speech and showed them where they were both in the right, and wound up by saying:

"You are both in the right in some ways and wrong in others. Therefore, I will say that you both are equally in the right."

When they heard this decision, they saw that the turtle was right, and gave him a long cheer for the wisdom displayed by him. The whole tribe saw that had it not been for this wise decision there would have been a great shedding of blood in the tribe. So they voted him as their judge, and the chief, being so well pleased with him, gave to him his only daughter in marriage.

The daughter of the chief was the most beautiful maiden of the Chippewa nation, and young men from other tribes traveled hundreds of miles for an opportunity to make love to her, and try to win her for a wife. It was all to no purpose. She would accept no one, only him whom her father would select for her. The turtle was very homely, but as he was prudent and wise, the father chose him, and she accepted him.

The young men of the tribe were very jealous, but their jealousy was

MARIE L. MCLAUGHLIN

all to no purpose. She married the turtle. The young men would make sport of the chief's son-in-law. They would say to him: "How did you come to have so flat a stomach?" The turtle answered them, saying:

"My friends, had you been in my place, you too would have flat stomachs. I came by my flat stomach in this way: The Chippewas and Sioux had a great battle, and the Sioux, too numerous for the Chippewas, were killing them off so fast that they had to run for their lives. I was on the Chippewa side and some of the Sioux were pressing five of us, and were gaining on us very fast. Coming to some high grass, I threw myself down flat on my face, and pressed my stomach close to the ground, so the pursuers could not see. They passed me and killed the four I was with. After they had gone back, I arose and lo! my stomach was as you see it now. So hard had I pressed to the ground that it would not assume its original shape again."

After he had explained the cause of his deformity to them, they said: "The Turtle is brave. We will bother him no more." Shortly after this the Sioux made an attack upon the Chippewas, and every one deserted the village. The Turtle could not travel as fast as the rest and was left behind. It being an unusually hot day in the fall, the Turtle grew very thirsty and sleepy. Finally scenting water, he crawled towards the point from whence the scent came, and coming to a large lake jumped in and had a bath, after which he swam towards the center and dived down, and finding some fine large rocks at the bottom, he crawled in among them and fell asleep. He had his sleep out and arose to the top.

Swimming to shore he found it was summer. He had slept all winter. The birds were singing, and the green grass and leaves gave forth a sweet odor.

He crawled out and started out looking for the Chippewa camp. He came upon the camp several days after he had left his winter quarters, and going around in search of his wife, found her at the extreme edge of the village. She was nursing her baby, and as he asked to see it, she showed it to him. When he saw that it was a lovely baby and did not resemble him in any respect, he got angry and went off to a large lake, where he contented himself with catching flies and insects and living on seaweed the remainder of his life.

The Man and the Oak

There once lived a Sioux couple who had two children, a boy and a girl. Every fall this family would move away from the main camp and take up their winter quarters in a grove of timber some distance from the principal village. The reason they did this was that he was a great hunter and where a village was located for the winter the game was usually very scarce. Therefore, he always camped by himself in order to have an abundance of game adjacent to his camp.

All summer he had roamed around following the tribe to wherever their fancy might take them. During their travels this particular year there came to the village a strange girl who had no relatives there. No one seemed very anxious to take her into their family, so the great hunter's daughter, taking a fancy to the poor girl, took her to their home and kept her. She addressed her as sister, and the parents, on account of their daughter, addressed her as daughter.

This strange girl became desperately in love with the young man of the family, but being addressed as daughter by the parents, she could not openly show her feelings as the young man was considered her brother.

In the fall when the main village moved into a large belt of timber for their winter quarters, the hunter moved on to another place two days' travel from the main winter camp, where he would not be disturbed by any other hunters.

The young man had a tent by himself, and it was always kept nice and clean by his sister, who was very much attached to him. After a long day's hunt in the woods, he would go into his tent and lie down to rest, and when his supper was ready his sister would say, "My brother is so tired. I will carry his supper to him."

Her friend, whom she addressed as sister, would never go into the young man's tent. Along towards spring there came one night into the young man's tent a woman. She sat down by the door and kept her face covered so that it was hidden from view. She sat there a long time and finally arose and went away. The young man could not imagine who this could be. He knew that it was a long distance from the village and could not make out where the woman could have come from. The next night the woman came again and this time she came a little nearer to where the young man lay. She sat down and kept her face covered as before. Neither spoke a word. She sat there for a long time and then arose and departed. He was very much puzzled over the actions of this woman and decided to ascertain on her next visit who she was.

He kindled a small fire in his tent and had some ash wood laid on it so as to keep fire a long time, as ash burns very slowly and holds fire a long time.

The third night the woman came again and sat down still nearer his bed. She held her blanket open just a trifle, and he, catching up one of the embers, flashed it in her face; jumping up she ran hurriedly out of the tent. The next morning he noticed that his adopted sister kept her face hidden with her blanket. She chanced to drop her blanket while in the act of pouring out some soup, and when she did so he noticed a large burned spot on her cheek.

He felt so sorry for what he had done that he could eat no breakfast, but went outside and lay down under an oak tree. All day long he lay there gazing up into the tree, and when he was called for supper he refused, saying that he was not hungry, and for them not to bother him, as he would soon get up and go to bed. Far into the night he lay thus, and when he tried to arise he could not, as a small oak tree grew through the center of his body and held him fast to the ground.

In the morning when the family awoke they found the girl had disappeared, and on going outside the sister discovered her brother held fast to the earth by an oak tree which grew very rapidly. In vain were the best medicine men of the tribe sent for. Their medicine was of no avail. They said: "If the tree is cut down the young man will die."

The sister was wild with grief, and extending her hands to the sun, she cried: "Great Spirit, relieve my suffering brother. Any one who releases him I will marry, be he young, old, homely or deformed."

Several days after the young man had met with the mishap, there came to the tent a very tall man, who had a bright light encircling his body. "Where is the girl who promised to marry any one who would release her brother?" "I am the one," said the young man's sister. "I am the all-powerful lightning and thunder. I see all things and can kill at one stroke a whole tribe. When I make my voice heard the rocks shake loose and go rattling down the hillsides. The brave warriors cower shivering under some shelter at the sound of my voice. The girl whom you had adopted as your sister was a sorceress. She bewitched your brother because he would not let her make love to him. On my way here I met her traveling towards the west, and knowing what she had done, I struck her with one of my blazing swords, and she lies there now a heap of ashes. I will now release your brother."

So saying he placed his hand on the tree and instantly it crumbled to ashes. The young man arose, and thanked his deliverer.

Then they saw a great black cloud approaching, and the man said: "Make ready, we shall go home on that cloud." As the cloud approached near to the man who stood with his bride, it suddenly lowered and enveloped them and with a great roar and amidst flashes of lightning and loud peals of thunder the girl ascended and disappeared into the west with her Thunder and Lightning husband.

Story of the Two Young Friends

There were once in a very large Indian camp two little boys who were fast friends. One of the boys, "Chaske" (meaning first born), was the son of a very rich family, and was always dressed in the finest of clothes of Indian costume. The other boy, "Hake" (meaning last born), was an orphan and lived with his old grandmother, who was very destitute, and consequently could not dress the boy in fine raiment. So poorly was the boy dressed that the boys who had good clothes always tormented him and would not play in his company.

Chaske did not look at the clothes of any boy whom he chose as a friend, but mingled with all boys regardless of how they were clad, and would study their dispositions. The well dressed he found were vain and conceited. The fairly well dressed he found selfish and spiteful. The poorly clad he found to be generous and truthful, and from all of them he chose "Hake" for his "Koda" (friend). As Chaske was the son of the leading war chief he was very much sought after by the rest of the boys, each one trying to gain the honor of being chosen for the friend and companion of the great chief's son; but, as I have before said, Chaske carefully studied them all and finally chose the orphan Hake.

It was a lucky day for Hake when he was chosen for the friend and companion of Chaske. The orphan boy was taken to the lodge of his friend's parents and dressed up in fine clothes and moccasins. (When the Indians' sons claim any one as their friend, the friend thus chosen is adopted into the family as their own son).

Chaske and Hake were inseparable. Where one was seen the other was not far distant. They played, hunted, trapped, ate and slept together. They would spend most of the long summer days hunting in the forests.

Time went on and these two fast friends grew up to be fine specimens of their tribe. When they became the age to select a sweetheart they would go together and make love to a girl. Each helping the other to win the affection of the one of his choice. Chaske loved a girl who was the daughter of an old medicine man. She was very much courted by the other young men of the tribe, and many a horse loaded with robes and fine porcupine work was tied at the medicine man's tepee in offering for the hand of his daughter, but the horses, laden as when tied there, were turned loose, signifying that the offer was not accepted.

The girl's choice was Chaske's friend Hake. Although he had never made love to her for himself, he had always used honeyed words to her and was always loud in his praises for his friend Chaske. One night the two friends had been to see the girl, and on their return Chaske was very quiet, having nothing to say and seemingly in deep study. Always of a bright, jolly and amiable disposition, his silence and moody spell grieved his friend very much, and he finally spoke to Chaske, saying: "Koda, what has come over you? You who were always so jolly and full of fun? Your silence makes me grieve for you and I do not know what you are feeling so downhearted about. Has the girl said anything to you to make you feel thus?"

"Wait, friend," said Chaske, "until morning, and then I will know how to answer your inquiry. Don't ask me anything more tonight, as my heart is having a great battle with my brain."

Hake bothered his friend no more that night, but he could not sleep. He kept wondering what "Pretty Feather" (the girl whom his friend loved) could have said to Chaske to bring such a change over him. Hake never suspected that he himself was the cause of his friend's sorrow, for never did he have a thought that it was himself that Pretty Feather loved.

The next morning after they had eaten breakfast, Chaske proposed that they should go out on the prairies, and see if they would have the good luck to kill an antelope. Hake went out and got the band of horses, of which there were over a hundred. They selected the fleetest two in the herd, and taking their bows and arrows, mounted and rode away towards the south.

Hake was overjoyed to note the change in his friend. His oldtime jollity had returned. They rode out about five miles, and scaring up a drove of antelope they started in hot pursuit, and as their horses were very fleet of foot soon caught up to the drove, and each singling out his choice quickly dispatched him with an arrow. They could easily have killed more of the antelope, but did not want to kill them just for sport, but for food, and knowing that they had now all that their horses could pack home, they dismounted and proceeded to dress their kill.

After each had finished packing the kill on his horse, Chaske said: "Let us sit down and have a smoke before we start back. Besides, I have something to tell you which I can tell better sitting still than I can riding along." Hake came and sat down opposite his friend, and while they smoked Chaske said:

"My friend, we have been together for the last twenty years and I have yet the first time to deceive you in any way, and I know I can truthfully say the same of you. Never have I known you to deceive me nor tell me an untruth. I have no brothers or sisters. The only brother's love I know is yours. The only sister's love I will know will be Pretty Feather's, for brother, last night she told me she loved none but you and would marry you and you only. So, brother, I am going to take my antelope to my sister-in-law's tent and deposit it at her door. Then she will know that her wish will be fulfilled. I thought at first that you had been playing traitor to me and had been making love to her for yourself, but when she explained it all to me and begged me to intercede for her to you, I then knew that I had judged you wrongfully, and that, together with my lost love, made me so quiet and sorrowful last night. So now, brother, take the flower of the nation for your wife, and I will be content to continue through life a lonely bachelor, as never again can I give any woman the place which Pretty Feather had in my heart."

Their pipes being smoked out they mounted their ponies and Chaske started up in a clear, deep voice the beautiful love song of Pretty Feather and his friend Hake.

Such is the love between two friends, who claim to be as brothers among the Indians. Chaske gave up his love of a beautiful woman for a man who was in fact no relation to him.

Hake said, "I will do as you say, my friend, but before I can marry the medicine man's daughter, I will have to go on the warpath and do some brave deed, and will start in ten days." They rode towards home, planning which direction they would travel, and as it was to be their first experience on the warpath, they would seek advice from the old warriors of the tribe.

On their arrival at the village Hake took his kill to their own tent, while Chaske took his to the tent of the Medicine Man, and deposited it at the door and rode off towards home.

The mother of Pretty Feather did not know whether to take the offering or not, but Pretty Feather, seeing by this offering that her most cherished wish was to be granted, told her mother to take the meat and cook it and invite the old women of the camp to a feast in honor of the son-in-law who was soon to keep them furnished with plenty of meat. Hake and his friend sought out all of the old warriors and gained all the information they desired. Every evening Hake visited his intended wife and many happy evenings they spent together.

The morning of the tenth day the two friends left the village and turned their faces toward the west where the camps of the enemy are more numerous than in any other direction. They were not mounted and therefore traveled slowly, so it took about ten days of walking before they saw any signs of the enemy. The old warriors had told them of a thickly wooded creek within the enemies' bounds. The old men said, "That creek looks the ideal place to camp, but don't camp there by any means, because there is a ghost who haunts that creek, and any one who camps there is disturbed all through the night, and besides they never return, because the ghost is Wakan (holy), and the enemies conquer the travelers every time." The friends had extra moccasins with them and one extra blanket, as it was late in the fall and the nights were very cold.

They broke camp early one morning and walked all day. Along towards evening, the clouds which had been threatening all day, hurriedly opened their doors and down came the snowflakes thick and fast. Just before it started snowing the friends had noticed a dark line about two miles in advance of them. Chaske spoke to his friend and said: "If this storm continues we will be obliged to stay overnight at Ghost Creek, as I noticed it not far ahead of us, just before the storm set in." "I noticed it also," said Hake. "We might as well entertain a ghost all night as to lie out on these open prairies and freeze to death." So they decided to run the risk and stay in the sheltering woods of Ghost Creek. When they got to the creek it seemed as if they had stepped inside a big tepee, so thick was the brush and timber that the wind could not be felt at all. They hunted and found a place where the brush was very thick and the grass very tall. They quickly pulled the tops of the nearest willows together and by intertwining the ends made them fast, and throwing their tent robe over this, soon had a cosy tepee in which to sleep. They started their fire and cooked some dried buffalo meat and buffalo tallow, and were just about to eat their supper when a figure of a man came slowly in through the door and sat down near where he had entered. Hake, being the one who was doing the cooking, poured out some tea into his own cup, and putting a piece of pounded meat and marrow into a small plate, placed it before the stranger, saying: "Eat, my friend, we are on the warpath and do not carry much of a variety of food with us, but I give you the best we have."

The stranger drew the plate towards him, and commenced eating ravenously. He soon finished his meal and handed the dish and cup back. He had not uttered a word so far. Chaske filled the pipe and handed it to him. He smoked for a few minutes, took one last draw from the pipe and handed it back to Chaske, and then he said: "Now, my friends, I am not a living man, but the wandering spirit of a once great warrior, who was killed in these woods by the enemy whom you two brave young men are now seeking to make war upon. For years I have been roaming these woods in hopes that I might find some one brave enough to stop and listen to me, but all who have camped here in the past have run away at my approach or fired guns or shot arrows at me. For such cowards as these I have always found a grave. They never returned to their homes. Now I have found two brave men whom I can tell what I want done, and if you accomplish what I tell you to do, you will return home with many horses and some scalps dangling from your belts. Just over this range of hills north of us, a large village is encamped for the winter. In that camp is the man who laid in ambush and shot me, killing me before I could get a chance to defend myself. I want that man's scalp, because he has been the cause of my wanderings for a great many years. Had he killed me on the battlefield my spirit would have at once joined my brothers in the happy hunting grounds, but being killed by a coward, my spirit is doomed to roam until I can find some brave man who will kill this coward and bring me his scalp. This is why I have tried every party who have camped here to listen to me, but as I have said before, they were all cowards. Now, I ask you two brave young men, will you do this for me?"

"We will," said the friends in one voice. "Thank you, my boys. Now, I know why you came here, and that one of you came to earn his feathers by killing an enemy, before he would marry; the girl he is to marry is my granddaughter, as I am the father of the great Medicine Man. In the morning there will pass by in plain sight of here a large party. They will chase the buffalo over on that flat. After they have passed an old man leading a black horse and riding a white one will come by on the trail left by the hunting party. He will be driving about a hundred horses, which he will leave over in the next ravine. He will then proceed to the hunting grounds and get meat from the different hunters. After the hunters have all gone home he will come last, singing the praises of the ones who gave him the meat. This man you must kill and scalp, as he is the one I want killed. Then take the white and black horse and each mount and go to the hunting grounds. There you will see two of the enemy riding about picking up empty shells. Kill and scalp these two and each take a scalp and come over to the high knoll and I will show you where the horses are, and as soon as you hand me the old man's scalp I will disappear and you will see me no more. As soon as I disappear, it will start in snowing. Don't be afraid as the snow will cover your trail, but nevertheless, don't stop traveling for three days and nights, as these people will suspect that some of your tribe have done this, and they will follow you until you cross your own boundary lines."

When morning came, the two friends sat in the thick brush and watched a large party pass by their hiding place. So near were they that the friends could hear them laughing and talking. After the hunting party had passed, as the spirit had told them, along came the old man, driving a large band of horses and leading a fine looking coal black horse. The horse the old man was riding was as white as snow. The friends crawled to a little brush covered hill and watched the chase after the shooting had ceased. The friends knew it would not be long before the return of the party, so they crawled back to their camp and hurriedly ate some pounded meat and drank some cherry tea. Then they took down their robe and rolled it up and got everything in readiness for a hurried flight with the horses. Scarcely had they got everything in readiness when the party came by, singing their song of the chase. When they had all gone the friends crawled down to the trail and lay waiting for the old man. Soon they heard him singing. Nearer and nearer came the sounds of the song until at last at a bend in the road, the old man came into view. The two friends arose and advanced to meet him. On he came still singing. No doubt he mistook them for some of his own people. When he was very close to them they each stepped to either side of him and before he could make an outcry they pierced his cowardly old heart with two arrows. He had hardly touched the ground when they both struck him with their bows, winning first and second honors by striking an enemy after he has fallen. Chaske having won first honors, asked his friend to perform the scalping deed, which he did. And wanting to be sure that the spirit would get full revenge, took the whole scalp, ears and all, and tied it to his belt. The buffalo beef which the old man had packed upon the black horse, they threw on the top of the old man. Quickly mounting the two horses, they hastened out across the long flat towards the hunting grounds. When they came in sight of the grounds there they saw two men riding about from place to place. Chaske took after the one on the right, Hake the one on the left. When the two men saw these two strange men riding like the wind towards them, they turned their horses to retreat towards the hills, but the white and the black were the swiftest of the tribe's horses, and quickly overtook the two fleeing men. When they came close to the enemy they strung their arrows onto the bowstring and drove them through the two fleeing hunters. As they were falling they tried to shoot, but being greatly exhausted, their bullets whistled harmlessly over the heads of the two friends. They scalped the two enemies and took their guns and ammunition, also secured the two horses and started for the high knoll. When they arrived at the place, there stood the spirit. Hake presented him with the old man's scalp and then the spirit showed them the large band of horses, and saying, "Ride hard and long," disappeared and was seen no more by any war parties, as he was thus enabled to join his forefathers in the happy hunting grounds.

The friends did as the spirit had told them. For three days and three nights they rode steadily. On the fourth morning they came into their own boundary. From there on they rode more slowly, and let the band of horses rest and crop the tops of long grass. They would stop occasionally, and while one slept the other kept watch. Thus they got fairly well rested before they came in sight of where their camp had stood when they had left. All that they could see of the once large village was the lone tent of the great Medicine Man. They rode up on to a high hill and farther on towards the east they saw smoke from a great many tepees. They then knew that something had happened and that the village had moved away.

"My friend," said Chaske, "I am afraid something has happened to the Medicine Man's lodge, and rather than have you go there, I will go alone and you follow the trail of our party and go on ahead with the horses. I will take the black and the white horses with me and I will follow on later, after I have seen what the trouble is."

"Very well, my friend, I will do as you say, but I am afraid something has happened to Pretty Feather." Hake started on with the horses, driving them along the broad trail left by the hundreds of travois. Chaske made slowly towards the tepee, and stopping outside, stood and listened. Not a sound could he hear. The only living thing he saw was Pretty Feather's spotted horse tied to the side of the tent. Then he knew that she must be dead. He rode off into the thick brush and tied his two horses securely. Then he came back and entered the tepee. There on a bed of robes lay some one apparently dead. The body was wrapped in blankets and robes and bound around and around with parfleche ropes. These he carefully untied and unwound. Then he unwrapped the robes and blankets and when he uncovered the face, he saw, as he had expected to, the face of his lost love, Pretty Feather. As he sat gazing on her beautiful young face, his heart ached for his poor friend. He himself had loved and lost this beautiful maiden, and now his friend who had won her would have to suffer the untold grief which he had suffered.

What was that? Could it have been a slight quivering of the nostrils that he had seen, or was it mad fancy playing a trick on him? Closer he drew to her face, watching intently for another sign. There it was again, only this time it was a long, deep drawn breath. He arose, got some water and taking a small stick slowly forced open her mouth and poured some into it. Then he took some sage, dipped it into the water and sprinkled a little on her head and face. There were many parfleche bags piled around the tepee, and thinking he might find some kind of medicine roots which he could use to revive her he started opening them one after the other. He had opened three and was just opening the fourth, when a voice behind him asked: "What are you looking for?" Turning quickly, he saw Pretty Feather looking at him. Overjoyed, he cried, "What can I do so that you can get up and ride to the village with me? My friend and I just returned with a large band of horses and two scalps. We saw this tent and recognized it. My friend wanted to come, but I would not let him, as I feared if he found anything had happened to you he would do harm to himself, but now he will be anxious for my return, so if you will tell me what you need in order to revive you, I will get it, and we can then go to my friend in the village." "At the foot of my bed you will find a piece of eagle fat. Build a fire and melt it for me. I will drink it and then we can go."

Chaske quickly started a fire, got out the piece of fat and melted it. She drank it at one draught, and was about to arise when she suddenly said: "Roll me up quick and take the buffalo hair rope and tie it about my spotted horse's neck; tie his tail in a knot and tie him to the door. Then run and hide behind the trees. There are two of the enemy coming this way."

Chaske hurriedly obeyed her orders, and had barely concealed himself behind the trees, when there came into view two of the enemy. They saw the horse tied to the door of the deserted tent, and knew that some dead person occupied the tepee, so through respect for the dead, they turned out and started to go through the brush and trees, so as not to pass the door. (The Indians consider it a bad omen to pass by the door of a tepee occupied by a dead body, that is, while in the enemy's country).

So by making this detour they traveled directly towards where Chaske was concealed behind the tree. Knowing that he would be discovered, and there being two of them, he knew the only chance he had was for him to kill one of them before they discovered him, then he stood a better chance at an even combat. On they came, little thinking that one of them would in a few minutes be with his forefathers.

Chaske noiselessly slipped a cartridge into the chamber of his gun, threw it into action and took deliberate aim at the smaller one's breast. A loud report rang out and the one he had aimed at threw up his arms and fell heavily forward, shot through the heart.

Reloading quickly Chaske stepped out from behind the tree. He could easily have killed the other from his concealed position, but, being a brave young man, he wanted to give his opponent a fair chance. The other had unslung his gun and a duel was then fought between the two lone combatants. They would spring from side to side like two great cats. Then advance one or two steps and fire. Retreat a few steps, spring to one side and fire again. The bullets whistled past their heads, tore up the earth beneath their feet, and occasionally one would hit its mark, only to cause a flesh wound.

Suddenly the enemy aimed his gun and threw it upon the ground. His ammunition was exhausted, and slowly folding his arms he stood facing his opponent, with a fearless smile upon his face, expecting the next moment to fall dead from a bullet from the rifle of Chaske. Not so. Chaske was too honorable and noble to kill an unarmed man, and especially one who had put up such a brave fight as had this man. Chaske advanced and picked up the empty gun. The Toka (enemy) drew from a scabbard at his belt a long bowie knife, and taking it by the point handed it, handle first, to Chaske. This signified surrender. Chaske scalped the dead Toka and motioned for his prisoner to follow him. In the meantime Pretty Feather had gotten up and stood looking at the duel. When she heard the first shot she jumped up and cut a small slit in the tent from which she saw the whole proceedings. Knowing that one or both of them must be wounded, she hurriedly got water and medicine roots, and when they came to the tent she was prepared to dress their wounds.

Chaske had a bullet through his shoulder and one through his hand. They were very painful but not dangerous. The prisoner had a bullet through his leg, also one through the muscle of his left arm. Pretty Feather washed and dressed their wounds, and Chaske went and brought the black and white horses and mounting Pretty Feather upon the white horse, and the prisoner on her spotted one, the three soon rode into the village, and there was a great cry of joy when it was known that Pretty Feather had come back to them again.

Hake, who was in his tent grieving, was told that his friend had returned and with him Pretty Feather. Hearing this good news he at once went to the Medicine Man's tent and found the Medicine Man busily dressing the wounds of his friend and a stranger. The old Medicine Man turned to Hake and said:

"Son-in-law, take your wife home with you. It was from grief at your absence that she went into a trance, and we, thinking she was dead, left her for such. Hadn't it been for your friend here, she would surely have been a corpse now. So take her and keep her with you always, and take as a present from me fifty of my best horses."

Hake and his beautiful bride went home, where his adopted mother had a fine large tent put up for them. Presents of cooking utensils, horses, robes and finely worked shawls and moccasins came from every direction, and last of all Chaske gave as a present to his friend the Toka man whom he had taken as prisoner. On presenting him with this gift, Chaske spoke thus:

"My friend, I present to you, that you may have him as a servant to look after your large band of horses, this man with whom I fought a two hours' duel, and had his ammunition lasted he would probably have conquered me, and who gave me the second hardest fight of my life. The hardest fight of my life was when I gave up Pretty Feather. You have them both. To the Toka (enemy) be kind, and he will do all your biddings. To Pretty Feather be a good husband."

So saying, Chaske left them, and true to his word, lived the remainder of his days a confirmed bachelor.

The Story of the Pet Crow

Once upon a time there came to a large village a plague of crows. So thick were they that the poor women were sorely tried keeping them out of their tepees and driving them away from their lines of jerked buffalo meat. Indeed they got so numerous and were such a great nuisance that the Chief finally gave orders to his camp criers or heralds to go out among the different camps and announce the orders of their Chief, that war should be made upon the crows to extermination; that their nests were to be destroyed and all eggs broken. The war of extermination was to continue until not a crow remained, except the youngest found was to be brought to him alive.

For a week the war on the crows continued. Thousands of dead crows were brought in daily, and at the end of the week not a bird of that species could be seen in the neighborhood. Those that escaped the deadly arrow of the warriors, flew away, never to return to those parts again.

At the end of the war made upon the crows, there was brought to the Chief's tepee the youngest found. Indeed, so young was the bird that it was only the great medicine of the Chief that kept him alive until he could hop about and find his own food. The Chief spent most of his time in his lodge teaching the young crow to understand and talk the language of the tribe. After the crow had mastered this, the Chief then taught him the languages of the neighboring tribes. When the crow had mastered these different languages the chief would send him on long journeys to ascertain the location of the camps of the different enemies.

When the crow would find a large Indian camp he would alight and hop about, pretending to be picking up scraps, but really keeping his ears open for anything he might hear. He would hang around all day, and at night when they would all gather in the large council tent (which always stood in the center of the village) to determine upon their next raid, and plan for a horse stealing trip, Mr. Crow was always nearby to hear all their plans discussed. He would then fly away to his master (the Chief) and tell him all that he had learned.

The Chief would then send a band of his warriors to lie in ambush for the raiding party, and, as the enemy would not suspect anything they would go blindly into the pitfall of death thus set for them. Thus the crow was the scout of this chief, whose reputation as a Wakan (Holy man) soon reached all of the different tribes. The Chief's warriors would intercept, ambush and annihilate every war party headed for his camp.

So, finally learning that they could not make war on this chief's people unbeknown to them, they gave up making war on this particular band. When meat was running low in the camp this chief would send the crow out to look for buffalo. When he discovered a herd he would return and report to his master; then the chief would order out the hunters and they would return laden with meat. Thus the crow kept the camp all the time informed of everything that would be of benefit to them.

One day the crow disappeared, over which there was great grief among the tribe. A week had passed away, when Mr. Crow reappeared. There was great rejoicing upon his return, but the crow was downcast and would not speak, but sat with a drooping head perched at the top of the chief's tepee, and refused all food that was offered to him.

In vain did the chief try to get the crow to tell him the cause of his silence and seeming grief. The crow would not speak until the chief said: "Well, I will take a few of my warriors and go out and try to ascertain what has happened to cause you to act as you do."

Upon hearing this, the crow said: "Don't go. I dreaded to tell you what I know to be a fact, as I have heard it from some great medicine men. I was traveling over the mountains west of here, when I spied three old men sitting at the top of the highest peak. I very cautiously dropped down behind a rock and listened to their talk. I heard your name mentioned by one of them, then your brother's name was mentioned. Then the third, who was the oldest, said: 'in three days from today the lightning will kill those two brothers whom all the nations fear.'"

Upon hearing what the crow stated the tribe became grief stricken. On the morning of the third day the chief ordered a nice tepee placed upon the highest point, far enough away from the village, so that the peals of thunder would not alarm the babies of the camp.

A great feast was given, and after the feasting was over there came in six young maidens leading the war horses of the two brothers. The horses were painted and decorated as if for a charge on the enemy. One maiden walked ahead of the chief's horse bearing in her hands the bow and arrows of the great warrior. Next came two maidens, one on either side of the prancing war steed, each holding a rein. Behind the chief's horse came the fourth maiden. Like the first, she bore in her hands the bow and arrows of the chief's brother. Then the fifth and sixth maidens each holding a rein, walked on either side of the prancing horse of the chief's brother. They advanced and circled the large gathering and finally stopped directly in front of the two brothers, who immediately arose and taking their bows and arrows vaulted lightly upon their war steeds, and singing their death song, galloped off amid a great cry of grief from the people who loved them most dearly.

Heading straight for the tepee that had been placed upon the highest point, adjacent to the village, they soon arrived at their destination and, dismounting from their horses, turned, waved their hands to their band, and disappeared within the tepee. Scarcely had they entered the lodge when the rumblings of distant thunder could be heard. Nearer, and nearer, came the sound, until at last the storm overspread the locality in all its fury. Flash upon flash of lightning burst forth from the heavens. Deafening peals of thunder followed each flash. Finally, one flash brighter than any of the others, one peal more deafening than those preceding it, and the storm had passed.

Sadly the warriors gathered together, mounted their horses and slowly rode to the tepee on the high point. Arriving there they looked inside the lodge and saw the two brothers lying cold and still in death, each holding the lariat of his favorite war horse. The horses also lay dead side by side in front of the tent. (From this came the custom of killing the favorite horse of a dead warrior at the burial of the owner).

As the Indians sadly left the hill to return home, they heard a noise at the top of the tepee, and looking up they saw the crow sitting on one of the splintered tepee poles. He was crying most pitifully, and as they rode off he flew up high in the air and his pitiful "caw" became fainter and fainter till at last they heard it no more. And from that day, the story goes, no crow ever goes near the village of that band of Indians.

The "Wasna" (Pemmican Man)
and the Unktomi (Spider)

O nce upon a time there appeared from out of a large belt of timber a man attired in the fat of the buffalo. On his head he wore the honeycomb part of the stomach. To this was attached small pieces of fat. The fat which covered the stomach he wore as a cloak. The large intestines he wore as leggings, and the kidney fat as his moccasins.

As he appeared he had the misfortune to meet "Unktomi" (spider) with his hundreds of starving children. Upon seeing the fat, Unktomi and his large family at once attacked the man, who, in order to save his life, started to run away, but so closely did Unktomi and his family pursue him that in order to make better time and also get a little better start, he threw off his head covering, which the Unktomi family hastily devoured, and were again closing in upon him. He then threw off his cloak and they devoured that, and were close upon him again, when he threw off his leggings. These were hastily eaten up, and, as they drew near to a lake, the man threw off the kidney fat, and, running to the edge of the lake, dived down into the water and kept beneath the surface, swimming to the opposite shore. After the Unktomi family had eaten the kidney fat they came to the water's edge, and the grease was floating on the surface of the water which they lapped up, until there was not a grease spot left floating on the surface.

The small morsels had only sharpened their appetites, and as they saw the man sitting on the opposite shore, Unktomi and his family proceeded around the lake and came upon two men sitting on the shore. Unktomi saw that the other man was "Wakapapi" (pounded beef). The family surrounded the two and Unktomi ordered them to fight. Fearing Unktomi and his large family, they at once commenced to fight and Pounded Meat was soon killed. The hungry family at once fell to eating him. So busy were they that none noticed the fat man sneak off and disappear.

When they had finished the pounded beef man they looked around to fall upon the fat man, but nowhere could he be seen. Unktomi said, "I will track him and when I find him, I will return for you, so stay here and await my return."

He followed the fat man's tracks until farther east on the shore of the lake he found the fat man in the act of skinning a deer, which he

MARIE L. MCLAUGHLIN

had killed. (He had held on to his bow and arrows when he jumped into the lake). "My," said Unktomi, "this will make a fine meal for my hungry children. I will go after them, so hurry and cut the meat up into small pieces so they each can have a piece."

"All right, go ahead and get your family," said Fat Man. During Unktomi's absence, the fat man hurriedly cut the meat up into small pieces and carried them up into a tree that stood near to the shore. When he had carried it all up he threw sand and dirt upon the blood, and so left no trace of the deer.

On the arrival of Unktomi and his family, no signs of the fat man or the deer could be found. They wandered about the spot looking for tracks which might lead them to where the fat man had cached the meat, as Unktomi said he could not have carried it very far. Now the fat man was up in the tree and sat watching them. The reflection of the tree was in the water, and some of the children going close to the shore, discovered it as they looked at the reflection. The fat man cut a piece of meat and extending it towards them, drew back his hand and put the meat into his mouth.

"Come quick, father, here he is eating the meat," said the children. Unktomi came and seeing the reflection, thought the fat man was down in the lake. "Wait, I will bring him up for you." So saying, he dived down, but soon arose without anything. Again and again he tried, but could not reach the bottom. He told the children to gather rock for him. These he tied around his neck and body, and dived down for the last time. The last the children saw of their father was the bubbles which arose to the surface of the lake. The rocks being too heavy for him, held him fast to the bottom, and some hungry fish soon made a feast out of the body of poor "Unktomi."

The Resuscitation of the Only Daughter

There once lived an old couple who had an only daughter. She was a beautiful girl, and was very much courted by the young men of the tribe, but she said that she preferred single life, and to all their heart-touching tales of deep affection for her she always had one answer. That was "No."

One day this maiden fell ill and day after day grew worse. All the best medicine men were called in, but their medicines were of no avail, and in two weeks from the day that she was taken ill she lay a corpse. Of course there was great mourning in the camp. They took her body several miles from camp and rolled it in fine robes and blankets, then they laid her on a scaffold which they had erected. (This was the custom of burial among the Indians). They placed four forked posts into the ground and then lashed strong poles lengthwise and across the ends and made a bed of willows and stout ash brush. This scaffold was from five to seven feet from the ground. After the funeral the parents gave away all of their horses, fine robes and blankets and all of the belongings of the dead girl. Then they cut their hair off close to their heads, and attired themselves in the poorest apparel they could secure.

When a year had passed the friends and relatives of the old couple tried in vain to have them set aside their mourning. "You have mourned long enough," they would say. "Put aside your mourning and try and enjoy a few more pleasures of this life while you live. You are both growing old and can't live very many more years, so make the best of your time." The old couple would listen to their advice and then shake their heads and answer: "We have nothing to live for. Nothing we could join in would be any amusement to us, since we have lost the light of our lives."

So the old couple continued their mourning for their lost idol. Two years had passed since the death of the beautiful girl, when one evening a hunter and his wife passed by the scaffold which held the dead girl. They were on their return trip and were heavily loaded down with game, and therefore could not travel very fast. About half a mile from the scaffold a clear spring burst forth from the side of a bank, and from this trickled a small stream of water, moistening the roots of the vegetation bordering its banks, and causing a growth of sweet green grass. At this spring the hunter camped and tethering his horses, at once set about helping his wife to erect the small tepee which they carried for convenience in traveling.

When it became quite dark, the hunter's dogs set up a great barking and growling. "Look out and see what the dogs are barking at," said the hunter to his wife. She looked out through the door and then drew back saying: "There is the figure of a woman advancing from the direction of the girl's scaffold." "I expect it is the dead girl; let her come, and don't act as if you were afraid," said the hunter. Soon they heard footsteps advancing and the steps ceased at the door. Looking down at the lower part of the door the hunter noticed a pair of small moccasins, and knowing that it was the visitor, said: "Whoever you are, come in and have something to eat."

At this invitation the figure came slowly in and sat down by the door with head covered and with a fine robe drawn tightly over the face. The woman dished up a fine supper and placing it before the visitor, said: "Eat, my friend, you must be hungry." The figure never moved, nor would it uncover to eat. "Let us turn our back towards the door and our visitor may eat the food," said the hunter. So his wife turned her back towards the visitor and made herself very busy cleaning the small pieces of meat that were hanging to the back sinews of the deer which had been killed. (This the Indians use as thread.) The hunter, filling his pipe, turned away and smoked in silence. Finally the dish was pushed back to the woman, who took it and after washing it, put it away. The figure still sat at the door, not a sound coming from it, neither was it breathing. The hunter at last said: "Are you the girl that was placed upon that scaffold two years ago?" It bowed its head two or three times in assent. "Are you going to sleep here tonight; if you are, my wife will make down a bed for you." The figure shook its head. "Are you going to come again tomorrow night to us?" It nodded assent.

For three nights in succession the figure visited the hunter's camp. The third night the hunter noticed that the figure was breathing. He saw one of the hands protruding from the robe. The skin was perfectly black and was stuck fast to the bones of the hand. On seeing this the hunter arose and going over to his medicine sack which hung on a pole, took down the sack and, opening it, took out some roots and mixing them with skunk oil and vermillion, said to the figure:

"If you will let us rub your face and hands with this medicine it will put new life into the skin and you will assume your complexion again and it will put flesh on you." The figure assented and the hunter rubbed the medicine on her hands and face. Then she arose and walked back to the scaffold. The next day the hunter moved camp towards the home village. That night he camped within a few miles of the village. When night came, the dogs, as usual, set up a great barking, and looking out, the wife saw the girl approaching.

When the girl had entered and sat down, the hunter noticed that the girl did not keep her robe so closely together over her face. When the wife gave her something to eat, the girl reached out and took the dish, thus exposing her hands, which they at once noticed were again natural. After she had finished her meal, the hunter said: "Did my medicine help you?" She nodded assent. "Do you want my medicine rubbed all over your body?" Again she nodded. "I will mix enough to rub your entire body, and I will go outside and let my wife rub it on for you." He mixed a good supply and going out left his wife to rub the girl. When his wife had completed the task she called to her husband to come in, and when he came in he sat down and said to the girl: "Tomorrow we will reach the village. Do you want to go with us?" She shook her head. "Will you come again to our camp tomorrow night after we have camped in the village?" She nodded her head in assent. "Then do you want to see your parents?" She nodded again, and arose and disappeared into the darkness.

Early the next morning the hunter broke camp and traveled far into the afternoon, when he arrived at the village. He instructed his wife to go at once and inform the old couple of what had happened. The wife did so and at sunset the old couple came to the hunter's tepee. They were invited to enter and a fine supper was served them. Soon after they had finished their supper the dogs of the camp set up a great barking. "Now she is coming, so be brave and you will soon see your lost daughter," said the hunter. Hardly had he finished speaking when she entered the tent as natural as ever she was in life. Her parents clung to her and smothered her with kisses.

They wanted her to return home with them, but she would stay with the hunter who had brought her back to life, and she married him, becoming his second wife. A short time after taking the girl for his wife, the hunter joined a war party and never returned, as he was killed on the battlefield.

A year after her husband's death she married again. This husband was also killed by a band of enemies whom the warriors were pursuing for stealing some of their horses. The third husband also met a similar fate to the first. He was killed on the field of battle.

She was still a handsome woman at the time of the third husband's death, but never again married, as the men feared her, saying she was holy, and that any one who married her would be sure to be killed by the enemy.

So she took to doctoring the sick and gained the reputation of being the most skilled doctor in the nation. She lived to a ripe old age and when she felt death approaching she had them take her to where she had rested once before, and crawling to the top of the newly erected scaffold, wrapped her blankets and robes about her, covered her face carefully, and fell into that sleep from which there is no more awakening.

The Story of the Pet Crane

There was once upon a time a man who did not care to live with his tribe in a crowded village, but preferred a secluded spot in the deep forest, there to live with his wife and family of five children. The oldest of the children (a boy) was twelve years of age, and being the son of a distinguished hunter, soon took to roaming through the forest in search of small game.

One day during his ramblings, he discovered a crane's nest, with only one young crane occupying it. No doubt some fox or traveling weasel had eaten the rest of the crane's brothers and sisters. The boy said to himself, "I will take this poor little crane home and will raise him as a pet for our baby. If I leave him here some hungry fox will be sure to eat the poor little fellow." He carried the young crane home and it grew to be nearly as tall as the boy's five-year-old sister.

Being brought up in a human circle, it soon grew to understand all the family said. Although it could not speak it took part in all the games played by the children. The father of the family was, as I have before mentioned, a great hunter. He always had a plentiful supply of deer, antelope, buffalo and beaver meats on hand, but there came a change. The game migrated to some other locality, where no deadly shot like "Kutesan" (Never Miss) would be around to annihilate their fast decreasing droves. The hunter started out early one morning in hopes of discovering some of the game which had disappeared as suddenly as though the earth had swallowed them. The hunter traveled the whole day, all to no purpose. It was late in the evening when he staggered into camp. He was nearly dead with fatigue. Hastily swallowing a cup of cherry bark tea (the only article of food they had in store), he at once retired and was soon in the sweet land of dreams. The children soon joined their father and the poor woman sat thinking how they could save their dear children from starvation. Suddenly out upon the night air rang the cry of a crane. Instantly the pet crane awoke, stepped outside and answered the call. The crane which had given the cry was the father of the pet crane, and learning from Mr. Fox of the starving condition of his son and his friends, he flew to the hunting grounds of the tribe, and as there had been a good kill that day, the crane found no trouble in securing a great quantity of fat. This he carried to the tent of the hunter and, hovering over the tent he suddenly let the fat drop to the earth and at once the pet crane picked it up and carried it to the woman.

Wishing to surprise the family on their awakening in the morning she got a good stick for a light, heaped up sticks on the dying embers, and started up a rousing fire and proceeded to melt or try out the fat, as melted fat is considered a favorite dish. Although busily occupied she kept her ears open for any strange noises coming out of the forest, there being usually some enemies lurking around. She held her pan in such a position that after the fat started to melt and quite a lot of the hot grease accumulated in the pan, she could plainly see the tent door reflected in the hot grease, as though she used a mirror.

When she had nearly completed her task, she heard a noise as though some footsteps were approaching. Instantly her heart began to beat a tattoo on her ribs, but she sat perfectly quiet, calling all her self-control into play to keep from making an outcry. This smart woman had already studied out a way in which to best this enemy, in case an enemy it should be. The footsteps, or noise, continued to advance, until at last the woman saw reflected in the pan of grease a hand slowly protruding through the tent door, and the finger pointed, as if counting, to the sleeping father, then to each one of the sleeping children, then to her who sat at the fire. Little did Mr. Enemy suppose that the brave woman who sat so composed at her fire, was watching every motion he was making. The hand slowly withdrew, and as the footsteps slowly died away, there rang out on the still night air the deep fierce howl of the prairie wolf. (This imitation of a prairie wolf is the signal to the war party that an enemy has been discovered by the scout whom they have sent out in advance). At once she aroused her husband and children. Annoyed at being so unceremoniously disturbed from his deep sleep, the husband crossly asked why she had awakened him so roughly. The wife explained what she had seen and heard. She at once pinned an old blanket around the crane's shoulders and an old piece of buffalo hide on his head for a hat or head covering. Heaping piles of wood onto the fire she instructed him to run around outside of the hut until the family returned, as they were going to see if they could find some roots to mix up with the fat. Hurriedly she tied her blanket around her middle, put her baby inside of it, and then grabbed her three year old son and packed him on her back. The father also hurriedly packed the next two and the older boy took care of himself.

Immediately upon leaving the tent they took three different directions, to meet again on the high hill west of their home. The reflection from the fire in the tent disclosed to them the poor pet crane running around the tent. It looked exactly like a child with its blanket and hat on.

Suddenly there rang out a score of shots and war whoops of the dreaded Crow Indians. Finding the tent deserted they disgustedly filed off and were swallowed up in the darkness of the deep forest.

The next morning the family returned to see what had become of their pet crane. There, riddled to pieces, lay the poor bird who had given up his life to save his dear friends.

White Plume

T here once lived a young couple who were very happy. The young man was noted throughout the whole nation for his accuracy with the bow and arrow, and was given the title of "Dead Shot," or "He who never misses his mark," and the young woman, noted for her beauty, was named Beautiful Dove.

One day a stork paid this happy couple a visit and left them a fine big boy. The boy cried "Ina, ina" (mother, mother). "Listen to our son," said the mother, "he can speak, and hasn't he a sweet voice?" "Yes," said the father, "it will not be long before he will be able to walk." He set to work making some arrows, and a fine hickory bow for his son. One of the arrows he painted red, one blue, and another yellow. The rest he left the natural color of the wood. When he had completed them, the mother placed them in a fine quiver, all worked in porcupine quills, and hung them up over where the boy slept in his fine hammock of painted moose hide.

At times when the mother would be nursing her son, she would look up at the bow and arrows and talk to her baby, saying: "My son, hurry up and grow fast so you can use your bow and arrows. You will grow up to be as fine a marksman as your father." The baby would coo and stretch his little arms up towards the bright colored quiver as though he understood every word his mother had uttered. Time passed and the boy grew up to a good size, when one day his father said: "Wife, give our son the bow and arrows so that he may learn how to use them." The father taught his son how to string and unstring the bow, and also how to attach the arrow to the string. The red, blue and yellow arrows, he told the boy, were to be used only whenever there was any extra good shooting to be done, so the boy never used these three until he became a master of the art. Then he would practice on eagles and hawks, and never an eagle or hawk continued his flight when the boy shot one of the arrows after him.

One day the boy came running into the tent, exclaiming: "Mother, mother, I have shot and killed the most beautiful bird I ever saw." "Bring it in, my son, and let me look at it." He brought the bird and upon examining it she pronounced it a different type of bird from any she had ever seen. Its feathers were of variegated colors and on its head was a topknot of pure white feathers. The father, returning, asked the boy with which arrow he had killed the bird. "With the red one," answered the boy. "I was so anxious to secure the pretty bird that, although I know I could have killed it with one of my common arrows, I wanted to be certain, so I used the red one." "That is right, my son," said the father. "When you have the least doubt of your aim, always use one of the painted arrows, and you will never miss your mark."

The parents decided to give a big feast in honor of their son killing the strange, beautiful bird. So a great many elderly women were called to the tent of Pretty Dove to assist her in making ready for the big feast. For ten days these women cooked and pounded beef and cherries, and got ready the choicest dishes known to the Indians. Of buffalo, beaver, deer, antelope, moose, bear, quail, grouse, duck of all kinds, geese and plover meats there was an abundance. Fish of all kinds, and every kind of wild fruit were cooked, and when all was in readiness, the heralds went through the different villages, crying out: "Ho-po, ho-po" (now all, now all), "Dead Shot and his wife, Beautiful Dove, invite all of you, young and old, to their tepee to partake of a great feast, given by them in honor of a great bird which their son has killed, and also to select for their son some good name which he will bear through life. So all bring your cups and wooden dishes along with your horn spoons, as there will be plenty to eat. Come, all you council men and chiefs, as they have also a great tent erected for you in which you hold your council."

Thus crying, the heralds made the circle of the village. The guests soon arrived. In front of the tent was a pole stuck in the ground and painted red, and at the top of the pole was fastened the bird of variegated colors; its wings stretched out to their full length and the beautiful white waving so beautifully from its topknot, it was the center of attraction. Half way up the pole was tied the bow and arrow of the young marksman. Long streamers of fine bead and porcupine work waved from the pole and presented a very striking appearance. The bird was faced towards the setting sun. The great chief and medicine men pronounced the bird "Wakan" (something holy).

When the people had finished eating they all fell in line and marched in single file beneath the bird, in order to get a close view of it. By the time this vast crowd had fully viewed the wonderful bird, the sun was just setting clear in the west, when directly over the rays of the sun appeared a cloud in the shape of a bird of variegated colors. The councilmen were called out to look at the cloud, and the head medicine man said that it was a sign that the boy would grow up to be a great chief and hunter, and would have a great many friends and followers.

This ended the feast, but before dispersing, the chief and councilmen bestowed upon the boy the title of White Plume.

One day a stranger came to the village, who was very thin and nearly starved. So weak was he that he could not speak, but made signs for something to eat. Luckily the stranger came to Dead Shot's tent, and as there was always a plentiful supply in his lodge, the stranger soon had a good meal served him. After he had eaten and rested he told his story.

"I came from a very great distance," said he. "The nations where I came from are in a starving condition. No place can they find any buffalo, deer nor antelope. A witch or evil spirit in the shape of a white buffalo has driven all the large game out of the country. Every day this white buffalo comes circling the village, and any one caught outside of their tent is carried away on its horns. In vain have the best marksmen of the tribe tried to shoot it. Their arrows fly wide off the mark, and they have given up trying to kill it as it bears a charmed life. Another evil spirit in the form of a red eagle has driven all the birds of the air out of our country. Every day this eagle circles above the village, and so powerful is it that anyone being caught outside of his tent is descended upon and his skull split open to the brain by the sharp breastbone of the Eagle. Many a marksman has tried his skill on this bird, all to no purpose.

"Another evil spirit in the form of a white rabbit has driven out all the animals which inhabit the ground, and destroyed the fields of corn and turnips, so the nation is starving, as the arrows of the marksmen have also failed to touch the white rabbit. Any one who can kill these three witches will receive as his reward, the choice of two of the most beautiful maidens of our nation. The younger one is the handsomer of the two and has also the sweetest disposition. Many young, and even old men, hearing of this (our chief's) offer, have traveled many miles to try their arrows on the witches, but all to no purpose. Our chief, hearing of your great marksmanship, sent me to try and secure your services to have you come and rid us of these three witches."

Thus spoke the stranger to the hunter. The hunter gazed long and thoughtfully into the dying embers of the camp fire. Then slowly his eyes raised and looked lovingly on his wife who sat opposite to him. Gazing on her beautiful features for a full minute he slowly dropped his gaze back to the dying embers and thus answered his visitor:

"My friend, I feel very much honored by your chief having sent such a great distance for me, and also for the kind offer of his lovely daughter in marriage, if I should succeed, but I must reject the great offer, as I can spare none of my affections to any other woman than to my queen whom you see sitting there."

White Plume had been listening to the conversation and when his father had finished speaking, said: "Father, I am a child no more. I have arrived at manhood. I am not so good a marksman as you, but I will go to this suffering tribe and try to rid them of their three enemies. If this man will rest for a few days and return to his village and inform them of my coming, I will travel along slowly on his trail and arrive at the village a day or two after he reaches there."

"Very well, my son," said the father, "I am sure you will succeed, as you fear nothing, and as to your marksmanship, it is far superior to mine, as your sight is much clearer and aim quicker than mine."

The man rested a few days and one morning started off, after having instructed White Plume as to the trail. White Plume got together what he would need on the trip and was ready for an early start the next morning. That night Dead Shot and his wife sat up away into the night instructing their son how to travel and warning him as to the different kinds of people he must avoid in order to keep out of trouble. "Above all," said the father, "keep a good look out for Unktomi (spider); he is the most tricky of all, and will get you into trouble if you associate with him."

White Plume left early, his father accompanying him for several miles. On parting, the father's last words were: "Look out for Unktomi, my son, he is deceitful and treacherous." "I'll look out for him, father;" so saying he disappeared over a hill. On the way he tried his skill on several hawks and eagles and he did not need to use his painted arrows to kill them, but so skillful was he with the bow and arrows that he could bring down anything that flew with his common arrows. He was drawing near to the end of his destination when he had a large tract of timber to pass through. When he had nearly gotten through the timber he saw an old man sitting on a log, looking wistfully up into a big tree, where sat a number of prairie chickens.

"Hello, grandfather, why are you sitting there looking so downhearted?" asked White Plume. "I am nearly starved, and was just wishing some one would shoot one of those chickens for me, so I could make a good meal on it," said the old man. "I will shoot one for you," said the young man. He strung his bow, placed an arrow on the string, simply seemed to raise the arrow in the direction of the chicken (taking no aim). Twang went out the bow, zip went the arrow and a chicken fell off the limb, only to get caught on another in its descent. "There is your chicken, grandfather."

"Oh, my grandson, I am too weak to climb up and get it. Can't you climb up and get it for me?" The young man, pitying the old fellow, proceeded to climb the tree, when the old man stopped him, saying: "Grandson, you have on such fine clothes, it is a pity to spoil them; you had better take them off so as not to spoil the fine porcupine work on them." The young man took off his fine clothes and climbed up into the tree, and securing the chicken, threw it down to the old man. As the young man was scaling down the tree, the old man said: "Iyashkapa, iyashkapa," (stick fast, stick fast). Hearing him say something, he asked, "What did you say, old man?" He answered, "I was only talking to myself." The young man proceeded to descend, but he could not move. His body was stuck fast to the bark of the tree. In vain did he beg the old man to release him. The old Unktomi, for he it was, only laughed and said: "I will go now and kill the evil spirits, I have your wonderful bow and arrows and I cannot miss them. I will marry the chief's daughter, and you can stay up in that tree and die there."

So saying, he put on White Plume's fine clothes, took his bow and arrows and went to the village. As White Plume was expected at any minute, the whole village was watching for him, and when Unktomi came into sight the young men ran to him with a painted robe, sat him down on it and slowly raising him up they carried him to the tent of the chief. So certain were they that he would kill the evil spirits that the chief told him to choose one of the daughters at once for his wife. (Before the arrival of White Plume, hearing of him being so handsome, the two girls had quarreled over which should marry him, but upon seeing him the younger was not anxious to become his wife.) So Unktomi chose the older one of the sisters, and was given a large tent in which to live. The younger sister went to her mother's tent to live, and the older was very proud, as she was married to the man who would save the nation from starvation. The next morning there was a great commotion in camp, and there came the cry that the white buffalo was coming. "Get ready, son-in-law, and kill the buffalo," said the chief.

Unktomi took the bow and arrows and shot as the buffalo passed, but the arrow went wide off its mark. Next came the eagle, and again he shot and missed. Then came the rabbit, and again he missed.

"Wait until tomorrow, I will kill them all. My blanket caught in my bow and spoiled my aim." The people were very much disappointed, and the chief, suspecting that all was not right, sent for the young man who had visited Dead Shot's tepee. When the young man arrived, the chief asked: "Did you see White Plume when you went to Dead Shot's camp?" "Yes, I did, and ate with him many times. I stayed at his father's tepee all the time I was there," said the young man. "Would you recognize him if you saw him again?" asked the chief. "Any one who had but one glimpse of White Plume would surely recognize him when he saw him again, as he is the most handsome man I ever saw," said the young man.

"Come with me to the tent of my son-in-law and take a good look at him, but don't say what you think until we come away." The two went to the tent of Unktomi, and when the young man saw him he knew it was not White Plume, although it was White Plume's bow and arrows that hung at the head of the bed, and he also recognized the clothes as belonging to White Plume. When they had returned to the chief's tent, the young man told what he knew and what he thought. "I think this is some Unktomi who has played some trick on White Plume and has taken his bow and arrows and also his clothes, and hearing of your offer, is here impersonating White Plume. Had White Plume drawn the bow on the buffalo, eagle and rabbit today, we would have been rid of them, so I think we had better scare this Unktomi into telling us where White Plume is," said the young man.

"Wait until he tries to kill the witches again tomorrow," said the chief.

In the meantime the younger daughter had taken an axe and gone into the woods in search of dry wood. She went quite a little distance into the wood and was chopping a dry log. Stopping to rest a little she heard some one saying: "Whoever you are, come over here and chop this tree down so that I may get loose." Going to where the big tree stood, she saw a man stuck onto the side of the tree. "If I chop it down the fall will kill you," said the girl. "No, chop it on the opposite side from me, and the tree will fall that way. If the fall kills me, it will be better than hanging up here and starving to death," said White Plume, for it was he.

The girl chopped the tree down and when she saw that it had not killed the man, she said: "What shall I do now?" "Loosen the bark from the tree and then get some stones and heat them. Get some water and sage and put your blanket over me." She did as told and when the steam arose from the water being poured upon the heated rocks, the bark loosened from his body and he arose. When he stood up, she saw how handsome he was. "You have saved my life," said he. "Will you be my wife?" "I will," said she. He then told her how the old man had fooled him into this trap and took his bow and arrows, also his fine porcupine worked clothes, and had gone off, leaving him to die. She, in turn, told him all that had happened in camp since a man, calling himself White Plume, came there and married her sister before he shot at the witches, and when he came to shoot at them, missed every shot. "Let us make haste, as the bad Unktomi may ruin my arrows." They approached the camp and whilst White Plume waited outside, his promised wife entered Unktomi's tent and said: "Unktomi, White Plume is standing outside and he wants his clothes and bow and arrows." "Oh, yes, I borrowed them and forgot to return them; make haste and give them to him."

Upon receiving his clothes, he was very much provoked to find his fine clothes wrinkled and his bow twisted, while the arrows were twisted out of shape. He laid the clothes down, also the bows and arrows, and passing his hand over them, they assumed their right shapes again. The daughter took White Plume to her father's tent and upon hearing the story he at once sent for his warriors and had them form a circle around Unktomi's tent, and if he attempted to escape to catch him and tie him to a tree, as he (the chief) had determined to settle accounts with him for his treatment of White Plume, and the deception employed in winning the chief's eldest daughter. About midnight the guard noticed something crawling along close to the ground, and seizing him found it was Unktomi trying to make his escape before daylight, whereupon they tied him to a tree. "Why do you treat me thus," cried Unktomi, "I was just going out in search of medicine to rub on my arrows, so I can kill the witches." "You will need medicine to rub on yourself when the chief gets through with you," said the young man who had discovered that Unktomi was impersonating White Plume.

In the morning the herald announced that the real White Plume had arrived, and the chief desired the whole nation to witness his marksmanship. Then came the cry: "The White Buffalo comes." Taking his red arrow, White Plume stood ready. When the buffalo got about opposite him, he let his arrow fly. The buffalo bounded high in the air and came down with all four feet drawn together under its body, the red arrow having passed clear through the animal, piercing the buffalo's heart. A loud cheer went up from the village.

"You shall use the hide for your bed," said the chief to White Plume. Next came a cry, "the eagle, the eagle." From the north came an enormous red eagle. So strong was he, that as he soared through the air his wings made a humming sound as the rumble of distant thunder. On he came, and just as he circled the tent of the chief, White Plume bent his bow, with all his strength drew the arrow back to the flint point, and sent the blue arrow on its mission of death. So swiftly had the arrow passed through the eagle's body that, thinking White Plume had missed, a great wail went up from the crowd, but when they saw the eagle stop in his flight, give a few flaps of his wings, and then fall with a heavy thud into the center of the village, there was a greater cheer than before. "The red eagle shall be used to decorate the seat of honor in your tepee," said the chief to White Plume. Last came the white rabbit. "Aim good, aim good, son-in-law," said the chief. "If you kill him you will have his skin for a rug." Along came the white rabbit, and White Plume sent his arrow in search of rabbit's heart, which it found, and stopped Mr. Rabbit's tricks forever.

The chief then called all of the people together and before them all took a hundred willows and broke them one at a time over Unktomi's back. Then he turned him loose. Unktomi, being so ashamed, ran off into the woods and hid in the deepest and darkest corner he could find. This is why Unktomis (spiders) are always found in dark corners, and anyone who is deceitful or untruthful is called a descendant of the Unktomi tribe.

Story of Pretty Feathered Forehead

There was once a baby boy who came into the world with a small cluster of different colored feathers grown fast to his forehead. From this he derived his name, "Pretty Feathered Forehead." He was a very pleasant boy as well as handsome, and he had the respect of the whole tribe. When he had grown up to be a young man, he never, like other young men, made love to any of the tribe's beauties. Although they were madly in love with him, he never noticed any of them. There were many handsome girls in the different camps, but he passed them by.

One day he said: "Father, I am going on a visit to the Buffalo nation." The father gave his consent, and away went the son. The father and mother suspected the object of their son's visit to the Buffalo nation, and forthwith commenced preparing a fine reception for their intended daughter-in-law. The mother sewed together ten buffalo hides and painted the brave deeds of her husband on them. This she made into a commodious tent, and had work bags and fine robes and blankets put inside. This was to be the tent of their son and daughter-in-law. In a few weeks the son returned, bringing with him a beautiful Buffalo girl. The parents of the boy gave a big feast in honor of the occasion, and the son and his wife lived very happily together.

In the course of time a son came to the young couple, and the father was very proud of his boy. When the boy became a year old, the father said to his wife: "I am going for a visit to the Elk nation." The mother was very sad, as she knew her husband was going after another wife. He returned, bringing with him a very beautiful elk girl. When the Buffalo woman saw the elk girl she was very downcast and sad, but the husband said: "Don't be sad; she will do all the heavy work for you."

They lived quite happily together for a long time. The Elk girl also became the mother of a fine boy. The two boys had grown up large enough to play around. One day the Elk woman was tanning hides outside and the two boys were playing around near their mothers, when all at once the buffalo boy ran across the robe, leaving his tracks on the white robe which his step-mother had nearly completed. This provoked the elk woman and she gave vent to her feelings by scolding the boy: "You clumsy flat mouth, why couldn't you run around my work, instead of across it?" The buffalo cow standing in the door, heard every word that the elk woman had said, and when she heard her son called flat mouth it made her very angry, although she did not say a word to any one. She hurriedly gathered some of her belongings and, calling her son, she started off in a westerly direction.

The husband being absent on a hunting expedition did not return until late in the afternoon. Upon his return his oldest boy always ran out to meet him, but this time as the boy did not put in an appearance, the father feared that something had happened to the boy. So hurriedly going to his tent he looked around, but failing to see the boy or his mother, he asked his elk wife, where the boy and his mother were. The elk wife answered: "She took her boy on her back and started off in that direction," (pointing towards the west). "How long has she been gone?" "Since early morning." The husband hurriedly caught a fresh horse and, without eating anything, rode off in the direction taken by his buffalo wife and boy. Near dark he ascended a high hill and noticed a small tent down in the valley. It was a long distance down to the tent, so it was very late when he arrived there. He tethered his horse and went into the tent and found the boy and his mother fast asleep. Upon lying down beside them the boy awoke, and upon seeing his father, motioned to him to go outside with him.

On going outside the boy told his father that it would be useless for him to try and coax his mother to return, as she was too highly insulted by the elk wife to ever return. Then the boy told about what the elk wife had said and that she had called him flat mouth. "My mother is determined to return to her people, but if you want to follow us you may, and perhaps, after she has visited with her relatives a little while, you may induce her to return with you. In the morning we are going to start very early, and as the country we will travel through is very hard soil, I will stamp my feet hard so as to leave my tracks imprinted in the softest places, then you will be able to follow the direction we will take."

The two went into the tent and were soon fast asleep. The father, being very much fatigued, slept very soundly, and when he awoke the sun was beating down upon him. The mother and boy were nowhere to be seen. The tent had been taken down from over him so carefully that he had not been awakened. Getting his horse, he mounted and rode after the two who had left him sleeping. He had no trouble in following the trail, as the boy had stamped his feet hard and left his little tracks in the soft places.

MARIE L. MCLAUGHLIN

That evening he spied the little tent again and on getting to it found them both asleep. The boy awoke and motioned for his father to go outside. He again told his father that the next day's travel would be the hardest of all. "We will cross a great plain, but before we get there we will cross a sandy hollow. When you get to the hollow, look at my tracks; they will be deep into the sand, and in each track you will see little pools of water. Drink as much as you can, as this is the only chance you will get to have a drink, there being no water from there to the big ridge, and it will be dark by the time you get to the ridge. The relations of my mother live at that ridge and I will come and talk to you once more, before I leave you to join my mother's people."

Next morning, as before, he awoke to find himself alone. They had left him and proceeded on their journey. He mounted again and when he arrived at the sandy hollow, sure enough, there, deep in the sand, were the tracks of his son filled to the top with water. He drank and drank until he had drained the last one. Then he arose and continued on the trail, and near sundown he came in sight of their little tent away up on the side of the ridge. His horse suddenly staggered and fell forward dead, having died of thirst.

From there he proceeded on foot. When he got to where the tent stood he entered, only to find it empty. "I guess my son intends to come here and have his last talk with me," thought the father. He had eaten nothing for three days, and was nearly famished. He lay down, but the pangs of hunger kept sleep away. He heard footsteps outside and lay in readiness, thinking it might be an enemy. Slowly opening the covering of the door, his son looked in and seeing his father lying awake, drew back and ran off up the ridge, but soon returned bringing a small parcel with him. When he entered he gave the parcel to his father and said: "Eat, father; I stole this food for you, so I could not get very much." The father soon ate what his son had brought. When he had finished, the son said: "Tomorrow morning the relatives of my mother will come over here and take you down to the village. My mother has three sisters who have their work bags made identically the same as mother's. Were they to mix them up they could not each pick out her own without looking inside so as to identify them by what they have in them. You will be asked to pick out mother's work bag, and if you fail they will trample you to death. Next they will tell you to pick out my mother from among her sisters, and you will be unable to distinguish her from the other three, and if you fail they will bury you alive. The last they will try you on, in case you meet the first and second tests successfully, will be to require you to pick me out from my three cousins, who are as much like me as my reflection in the water. The bags you can tell by a little pebble I will place on my mother's. You can pick my mother out by a small piece of grass which I will put in her hair, and you can pick me out from my cousins, for when we commence to dance, I will shake my head, flop my ears and switch my tail. You must choose quickly, as they will be very angry at your success, and if you lose any time they will make the excuse that you did not know, that they may have an excuse to trample you to death."

The boy then left, after admonishing his father to remember all that he had told him. Early next morning the father heard a great rumbling noise, and going outside, he saw the whole hillside covered with buffalo. When he appeared they set up a loud bellowing and circled around him. One old bull came up and giving a loud snort, passed on by, looking back every few steps. The man, thinking he was to follow this one, did so, and the whole herd, forming a half circle around him, escorted him down the west side of the range out on to a large plain, where there stood a lone tree. To this tree the old bull led him and stopped when he reached the tree. A large rock at the foot of the tree served as a seat for the man. As soon as he was seated there came four female buffaloes, each bearing a large work box. They set the boxes down in a row in front of the man, and the herd crowded around closer in order to get a good view. The old bull came to the front and stood close to the bags, which had been taken out of the four boxes.

The man stood up, and looking at the bags, noticed a small pebble resting on the one next to the left end. Stepping over he pulled the bag towards him and secretly pushed the little pebble off the bag, so that no one would notice it. When they saw that he had selected the right one, they set up a terrific bellow.

Then came the four sisters and stood in a line before the man. Glancing along from the one on the right to the last one on the left, he stepped forward and placed his hand on the one next to the right. Thanks to his boy, if he hadn't put that little stem of grass on his mother's hair, the father could never have picked out his wife, as the four looked as much alike as four peas. Next came the four boy calves, and as they advanced they commenced dancing, and his son was shaking his head and flopping his ears and switching his tail. The father was going to pick out his boy, when a fainting spell took him, and as he sank to the ground the old bull

MARIE L. MCLAUGHLIN

sprang forward on top of him, and instantly they rushed upon him and he was soon trampled to a jelly. The herd then moved to other parts.

The elk wife concluded that something had happened to her husband and determined upon going in search of him. As she was very fleet of foot it did not take her long to arrive at the lone tree. She noticed the blood splashed on the base of the tree, and small pieces of flesh stamped into the earth. Looking closer, she noticed something white in the dust. Stooping and picking it out of the dust, she drew forth the cluster of different colored feathers which had been fastened to her husband's forehead. She at once took the cluster of feathers, and going to the east side of the ridge, heated stones and erected a wickieup, placed the feathers inside, and getting water, she sprinkled the stones, and this caused a thick vapor in the wickieup. She continued this for a long time, when she heard something moving inside the wickieup. Then a voice spoke up, saying: "Whoever you are, pour some more water on and I will be all right." So the woman got more water and poured it on the rocks. "That will do now, I want to dry off." She plucked a pile of sage and in handing it in to him, he recognized his elk wife's hand.

They went back home and shortly after the buffalo, hearing about him coming back to life, decided to make war on him and kill him and his wife, she being the one who brought him back to life. The woman, hearing of this, had posts set in the ground and a strong platform placed on top. When the buffalo came, her husband, her son and herself, were seated upon the bough platform, and the buffalo could not reach them. She flouted her red blanket in their faces, which made the buffalo wild with rage. The hunter's friends came to his rescue, and so fast were they killing the buffalo that they took flight and rushed away, never more to bother Pretty Feather Forehead.

The Four Brothers or Inyanhoksila
(Stone Boy)

Alone and apart from their tribe dwelt four orphan brothers. They had erected a very comfortable hut, although the materials used were only willows, hay, birch bark, and adobe mud. After the completion of their hut, the oldest brother laid out the different kinds of work to be done by the four of them. He and the second and third brothers were to do all the hunting, and the youngest brother was to do the house work, cook the meals, and keep plenty of wood on hand at all times.

As his older brothers would leave for their hunting very early every morning, and would not return till late at night, the little fellow always found plenty of spare time to gather into little piles fine dry wood for their winter use.

Thus the four brothers lived happily for a long time. One day while out gathering and piling up wood, the boy heard a rustling in the leaves and looking around he saw a young woman standing in the cherry bushes, smiling at him.

"Who are you, and where did you come from?" asked the boy, in surprise. "I am an orphan girl and have no relatives living. I came from the village west of here. I learned from rabbit that there were four orphan brothers living here all alone, and that the youngest was keeping house for his older brothers, so I thought I would come over and see if I couldn't have them adopt me as their sister, so that I might keep house for them, as I am very poor and have no relations, neither have I a home."

She looked so pitiful and sad that the boy thought to himself, "I will take her home with me, poor girl, no matter what my brothers think or say." Then he said to her: "Come on, tanke (sister). You may go home with me; I am sure my older brothers will be glad to have you for our sister."

When they arrived at the hut, the girl hustled about and cooked up a fine hot supper, and when the brothers returned they were surprised to see a girl sitting by the fire in their hut. After they had entered the youngest brother got up and walked outside, and a short time after the oldest brother followed him out. "Who is that girl, and where did she come from?" he asked his brother. Whereupon the brother told him the whole story. Upon hearing this the oldest brother felt very sorry for the poor orphan girl and going back into the hut he spoke to the girl, saying: "Sister, you are an orphan, the same as we; you have no relatives, no home. We will be your brothers, and our poor hut shall be your home. Henceforth call us brothers, and you will be our sister."

"Oh, how happy I am now that you take me as your sister. I will be to you all as though we were of the same father and mother," said the girl. And true to her word, she looked after everything of her brothers and kept the house in such fine shape that the brothers blessed the day that she came to their poor little hut. She always had an extra buckskin suit and two pairs of moccasins hanging at the head of each one's bed. Buffalo, deer, antelope, bear, wolf, wildcat, mountain lion and beaver skins she tanned by the dozen, and piled nicely in one corner of the hut.

When the Indians have walked a great distance and are very tired, they have great faith in painting their feet, claiming that paint eases the pain and rests their feet.

After their return from a long day's journey, when they would be lying down resting, the sister would get her paint and mix it with the deer tallow and rub the paint on her brother's feet, painting them up to their ankles. The gentle touch of her hands, and the soothing qualities of the tallow and paint soon put them into a deep, dreamless steep.

Many such kind actions on her part won the hearts of the brothers, and never was a full blood sister loved more than was this poor orphan girl, who had been taken as their adopted sister. In the morning when they arose, the sister always combed their long black silken scalp locks and painted the circle around the scalp lock a bright vermillion.

When the hunters would return with a goodly supply of beef, the sister would hurry and relieve them of their packs, hanging each one high enough from the ground so the prowling dogs and coyotes could not reach them. The hunters each had a post on which to hang his bow and flint head arrows. (Good hunters never laid their arrows on the ground, as it was considered unlucky to the hunter who let his arrows touch the earth after they had been out of the quiver). They were all perfectly happy, until one day the older brother surprised them all by saying: "We have a plentiful supply of meat on hand at present to last us for a week or so. I am going for a visit to the village west of us, so you boys all stay at home and help sister. Also gather as much wood as you can and I will be back again in four days. On my return we will resume our hunting and commence getting our year's supply of meat."

He left the next morning, and the last they saw of him was while he stood at the top of the long range of hills west of their home. Four days had come and gone and no sign of the oldest brother.

"I am afraid that our brother has met with some accident," said the sister. "I am afraid so, too," said the next oldest. "I must go and search for him; he may be in some trouble where a little help would get him out." The second brother followed the direction his brother had taken, and when he came to the top of the long range of hills he sat down and gazed long and steadily down into the long valley with a beautiful creek winding through it. Across the valley was a long plain stretching for miles beyond and finally ending at the foot of another range of hills, the counterpart of the one upon which he sat.

After noting the different landmarks carefully, he arose and slowly started down the slope and soon came to the creek he had seen from the top of the range. Great was his surprise on arriving at the creek to find what a difference there was in the appearance of it from the range and where he stood. From the range it appeared to be a quiet, harmless, laughing stream. Now he saw it to be a muddy, boiling, bubbling torrent, with high perpendicular banks. For a long time he stood, thinking which way to go, up or down stream. He had just decided to go down stream, when, on chancing to look up, he noticed a thin column of smoke slowly ascending from a little knoll. He approached the place cautiously and noticed a door placed into the creek bank on the opposite side of the stream. As he stood looking at the door, wondering who could be living in a place like that, it suddenly opened and a very old appearing woman came out and stood looking around her. Soon she spied the young man, and said to him: "My grandchild, where did you come from and whither are you bound?" The young man answered: "I came from east of this ridge and am in search of my oldest brother, who came over in this direction five days ago and who has not yet returned."

"Your brother stopped here and ate his dinner with me, and then left, traveling towards the west," said the old witch, for such she was. "Now, grandson, come across on that little log bridge up the stream there and have your dinner with me. I have it all cooked now and just stepped outside to see if there might not be some hungry traveler about, whom I could invite in to eat dinner with me." The young man went up the stream a little distance and found a couple of small logs which had been placed across the stream to serve as a bridge. He crossed over and went down to the old woman's dugout hut. "Come in grandson, and eat. I know you must be hungry."

The young man sat down and ate a real hearty meal. On finishing he arose and said: "Grandmother, I thank you for your meal and kindness to me. I would stay and visit with you awhile, as I know it must be very lonely here for you, but I am very anxious to find my brother, so I must be going. On my return I will stop with my brother and we will pay you a little visit."

"Very well, grandson, but before you go, I wish you would do me a little favor. Your brother did it for me before he left, and cured me, but it has come back on me again. I am subject to very severe pains along the left side of my backbone, all the way from my shoulder blade down to where my ribs attach to my backbone, and the only way I get any relief from the pain is to have some one kick me along the side." (She was a witch, and concealed in her robe a long sharp steel spike. It was placed so that the last kick they would give her, their foot would hit the spike and they would instantly drop off into a swoon, as if dead.)

"If I won't hurt you too much, grandmother, I certainly will be glad to do it for you," said the young man, little thinking he would be the one to get hurt.

"No, grandson, don't be afraid of hurting me; the harder you kick the longer the pain stays away." She laid down on the floor and rolled over on to her right side, so he could get a good chance to kick the left side where she said the pain was located.

As he moved back to give the first kick, he glanced along the floor and he noticed a long object wrapped in a blanket, lying against the opposite wall. He thought it looked strange and was going to stop and investigate, but just then the witch cried out as if in pain. "Hurry up, grandson, I am going to die if you don't hurry and start in kicking." "I can investigate after I get through with her," thought he, so he started in kicking and every kick he would give her she would cry: "Harder, kick harder." He had to kick seven times before he would get to the end of the pain, so he let out as hard as he could drive, and when he came to the last kick he hit the spike, and driving it through his foot, fell down in a dead swoon, and was rolled up in a blanket by the witch and placed beside his brother at the opposite side of the room.

When the second brother failed to return, the third went in search of the two missing ones. He fared no better than the second one, as he met the old witch who served him in a similar manner as she had his two brothers.

"Ha! Ha!" she laughed, when she caught the third, "I have only one more of them to catch, and when I get them I will keep them all here a year, and then I will turn them into horses and sell them back to their sister. I hate her, for I was going to try and keep house for them and marry the oldest one, but she got ahead of me and became their sister, so now I will get my revenge on her. Next year she will be riding and driving her brothers and she won't know it."

When the third brother failed to return, the sister cried and begged the last one not to venture out in search of them. But go he must, and go he did, only to do as his three brothers had done.

Now the poor sister was nearly distracted. Day and night she wandered over hills and through woods in hopes she might find or hear of some trace of them. Her wanderings were in vain. The hawks had not seen them after they had crossed the little stream. The wolves and coyotes told her that they had seen nothing of her brothers out on the broad plains, and she had given them up for dead.

One day, as she was sitting by the little stream that flowed past their hut, throwing pebbles into the water and wondering what she should do, she picked up a pure white pebble, smooth and round, and after looking at it for a long time, threw it into the water. No sooner had it hit the water than she saw it grow larger. She took it out and looked at it and threw it in again. This time it had assumed the form of a baby. She took it out and threw it in the third time and the form took life and began to cry: "Ina, ina" (mother, mother). She took the baby home and fed it soup, and it being an unnatural baby, quickly grew up to a good sized boy. At the end of three months he was a good big, stout youth. One day he said: "Mother, why are you living here alone? To whom do all these fine clothes and moccasins belong?" She then told him the story of her lost brothers. "Oh, I know now where they are. You make me lots of arrows. I am going to find my uncles." She tried to dissuade him from going, but he was determined and said: "My father sent me to you so that I could find my uncles for you, and nothing can harm me, because I am stone and my name is 'Stone Boy'."

The mother, seeing that he was determined to go, made a whole quiver full of arrows for him, and off he started. When he came to the old witch's hut, she was nowhere to be seen, so he pushed the door in and entered. The witch was busily engaged cooking dinner.

"Why, my dear grandchild, you are just in time for dinner. Sit down and we will eat before you continue your journey." Stone boy sat down and ate dinner with the old witch. She watched him very closely, but when she would be drinking her soup he would glance hastily around the room. Finally he saw the four bundles on the opposite side of the room, and he guessed at once that there lay his four uncles. When he had finished eating he took out his little pipe and filled it with "kinikinic," and commenced to smoke, wondering how the old woman had managed to fool his smart uncles. He couldn't study it out, so when he had finished his smoke he arose to pretend to go. When the old woman saw him preparing to leave, she said: "Grandson, will you kick me on the left side of my backbone. I am nearly dead with pain and if you kick me good and hard it will cure me." "All right, grandma," said the boy. The old witch lay down on the floor and the boy started in to kick. At the first kick he barely touched her. "Kick as hard as you can, grandson; don't be afraid you will hurt me, because you can't." With that Stone Boy let drive and broke two ribs. She commenced to yell and beg him to stop, but he kept on kicking until he had kicked both sides of her ribs loose from the backbone. Then he jumped on her backbone and broke it and killed the old witch.

He built a big fire outside and dragged her body to it, and threw her into the fire. Thus ended the old woman who was going to turn his uncles into horses.

Next he cut willows and stuck them into the ground in a circle. The tops he pulled together, making a wickieup. He then took the old woman's robes and blankets and covered the wickieup so that no air could get inside. He then gathered sage brush and covered the floor with a good thick bed of sage; got nice round stones and got them red hot in the fire, and placed them in the wickieup and proceeded to carry his uncles out of the hut and lay them down on the soft bed of sage. Having completed carrying and depositing them around the pile of rocks, he got a bucket of water and poured it on the hot rocks, which caused a great vapor in the little wickieup. He waited a little while and then listened and heard some breathing inside, so he got another bucket and poured that on also. After awhile he could hear noises inside as though some one were moving about. He went again and got the third bucket and after he had poured that on the rocks, one of the men inside said: "Whoever you are, good friend, don't bring us to life only to scald us to death again." Stone boy then said: "Are all of you alive?" "Yes," said the voice. "Well, come out," said the boy. And with that he threw off the robes and blankets, and a great cloud of vapor arose and settled around the top of the highest peak on the long range, and from that did Smoky Range derive its name.

The uncles, when they heard who the boy was, were very happy, and they all returned together to the anxiously waiting sister. As soon as they got home, the brothers worked hard to gather enough wood to last them all winter. Game they could get at all times of the year, but the heavy fall of snow covered most of the dry wood and also made it very difficult to drag wood through the deep snow. So they took advantage of the nice fall weather and by the time the snow commenced falling they had enough wood gathered to last them throughout the winter. After the snow fell a party of boys swiftly coasted down the big hill west of the brothers' hut. The Stone boy used to stand and watch them for hours at a time. His youngest uncle said: "Why don't you go up and coast with them?" The boy said: "They may be afraid of me, but I guess I will try once, anyway." So the next morning when the crowd came coasting, Stone boy started for the hill. When he had nearly reached the bottom of the coasting hill all of the boys ran off excepting two little fellows who had a large coaster painted in different colors and had little bells tied around the edges, so when the coaster was in motion the bells made a cheerful tinkling sound. As Stone boy started up the hill the two little fellows started down and went past him as though shot from a hickory bow.

When they got to the end of their slide, they got off and started back up the hill. It being pretty steep, Stone boy waited for them, so as to lend a hand to pull the big coaster up the hill. As the two little fellows came up with him he knew at once that they were twins, as they looked so much alike that the only way one could be distinguished from the other was by the scarfs they wore. One wore red, the other black. He at once offered to help them drag their coaster to the top of the hill. When they got to the top the twins offered their coaster to him to try a ride. At first he refused, but they insisted on his taking it, as they said they would sooner rest until he came back. So he got on the coaster and flew down the hill, only he was such an expert he made a zigzag course going down and also jumped the coaster off a bank about four feet high, which none of the other coasters dared to tackle. Being very heavy, however, he nearly smashed the coaster. Upon seeing this wonderful jump, and the zigzag course he had taken going down, the twins went wild with excitement and decided that they would have him take them down when he got back. So upon his arrival at the starting point, they both asked him at once to give them the pleasure of the same kind of a ride he had taken. He refused, saying: "We will break your coaster. I alone nearly smashed it, and if we all get on and make the same kind of a jump, I am afraid you will have to go home without your coaster."

MARIE L. MCLAUGHLIN

"Well, take us down anyway, and if we break it our father will make us another one." So he finally consented. When they were all seated ready to start, he told them that when the coaster made the jump they must look straight ahead. "By no means look down, because if you do we will go over the cut bank and land in a heap at the bottom of the gulch."

They said they would obey what he said, so off they started swifter than ever, on account of the extra weight, and so swiftly did the sleigh glide over the packed, frozen snow, that it nearly took the twins' breath away. Like an arrow they approached the jump. The twins began to get a little nervous. "Sit steady and look straight ahead," yelled Stone boy. The twin next to Stone boy, who was steering behind, sat upright and looked far ahead, but the one in front crouched down and looked into the coulee. Of course, Stone boy, being behind, fell on top of the twins, and being so heavy, killed both of them instantly, crushing them to a jelly.

The rest of the boys, seeing what had happened, hastened to the edge of the bank, and looking down, saw the twins laying dead, and Stone boy himself knocked senseless, lying quite a little distance from the twins. The boys, thinking that all three were killed, and that Stone boy had purposely steered the sleigh over the bank in such a way that it would tip and kill the twins, returned to the village with this report. Now, these twins were the sons of the head chief of the Buffalo Nation. So at once the chief and his scouts went over to the hill to see if the boys had told the truth.

When they arrived at the bank they saw the twins lying dead, but where was Stone boy? They looked high and low through the gulch, but not a sign of him could they find. Tenderly they picked up the dead twins and carried them home, then held a big council and put away the bodies of the dead in Buffalo custom.

A few days after this the uncles were returning from a long journey. When they drew near their home they noticed large droves of buffalo gathered on their side of the range. Hardly any buffalo ever ranged on this east side of the range before, and the brothers thought it strange that so many should so suddenly appear there now.

When they arrived at home their sister told them what had happened to the chief's twins, as her son had told her the whole story upon his arrival at home after the accident.

"Well, probably all the buffalo we saw were here for the council and funeral," said the older brother. "But where is my nephew?" (Stone boy) he asked his sister. "He said he had noticed a great many buffalo around lately and he was going to learn, if possible, what their object was," said the sister. "Well, we will wait until his return."

When Stone boy left on his trip that morning, before the return of his uncles, he was determined to ascertain what might be the meaning of so many buffalo so near the home of himself and uncles. He approached several bunches of young buffalo, but upon seeing him approaching they would scamper over the hills. Thus he wandered from bunch to bunch, scattering them all. Finally he grew tired of their cowardice and started for home. When he had come to within a half mile or so of home he saw an old shaggy buffalo standing by a large boulder, rubbing on it first one horn and then the other. On coming up close to him, the boy saw that the bull was so old he could hardly see, and his horns so blunt that he could have rubbed them for a year on that boulder and not sharpened them so as to hurt anyone.

"What are you doing here, grandfather?" asked the boy.

"I am sharpening my horns for the war," said the bull.

"What war?" asked the boy.

"Haven't you heard," said the old bull, who was so near sighted he did not recognize Stone boy. "The chief's twins were killed by Stone boy, who ran them over a cut bank purposely, and the chief has ordered all of his buffalo to gather here, and when they arrive we are going to kill Stone boy and his mother and his uncles."

"Is that so? When is the war to commence?"

"In five days from now we will march upon the uncles and trample and gore them all to death."

"Well, grandfather, I thank you for your information, and in return will do you a favor that will save you so much hard work on your blunt horns." So saying he drew a long arrow from his quiver and strung his bow, attached the arrow to the string and drew the arrow half way back. The old bull, not seeing what was going on, and half expecting some kind of assistance in his horn sharpening process, stood perfectly still. Thus spoke Stone boy:

"Grandfather, you are too old to join in a war now, and besides if you got mixed up in that big war party you might step in a hole or stumble and fall and be trampled to death. That would be a horrible death, so I will save you all that suffering by just giving you this." At this word he pulled the arrow back to the flint head and let it fly. True to his aim, the arrow went in behind the old bull's foreleg, and with such force

MARIE L. MCLAUGHLIN

was it sent that it went clear through the bull and stuck into a tree two hundred feet away.

Walking over to the tree, he pulled out his arrow. Coolly straightening his arrow between his teeth and sighting it for accuracy, he shoved it back into the quiver with its brothers, exclaiming: "I guess, grandpa, you won't need to sharpen your horns for Stone boy and his uncles."

Upon his arrival home he told his uncles to get to work building three stockades with ditches between and make the ditches wide and deep so they will hold plenty of buffalo. "The fourth fence I will build myself," he said.

The brothers got to work early and worked until very late at night. They built three corrals and dug three ditches around the hut, and it took them three days to complete the work. Stone boy hadn't done a thing towards building his fence yet, and there were only two days more left before the charge of the buffalo would commence. Still the boy didn't seem to bother himself about the fence. Instead he had his mother continually cutting arrow sticks, and as fast as she could bring them he would shape them, feather and head them. So by the time his uncles had their fences and corrals finished he had a thousand arrows finished for each of his uncles. The last two days they had to wait, the uncles joined him and they finished several thousand more arrows. The evening before the fifth day he told his uncles to put up four posts, so they could use them as seats from which to shoot.

While they were doing this, Stone boy went out to scout and see how things looked. At daylight he came hurriedly in saying, "You had better get to the first corral; they are coming." "You haven't built your fence, nephew." Whereupon Stone boy said: "I will build it in time; don't worry, uncle." The dust on the hillsides rose as great clouds of smoke from a forest fire. Soon the leaders of the charge came in sight, and upon seeing the timber stockade they gave forth a great snort or roar that fairly shook the earth. Thousands upon thousands of mad buffalo charged upon the little fort. The leaders hit the first stockade and it soon gave way. The maddened buffalo pushed forward by the thousands behind them; plunged forward, only to fall into the first ditch and be trampled to death by those behind them. The brothers were not slow in using their arrows, and many a noble beast went down before their deadly aim with a little flint pointed arrow buried deep in his heart.

The second stockade stood their charge a little longer than did the first, but finally this gave way, and the leaders pushed on through, only to fall into the second ditch and meet a similar fate to those in the first. The brothers commenced to look anxiously towards their nephew, as there was only one more stockade left, and the second ditch was nearly bridged over with dead buffalo, with the now thrice maddened buffalo attacking the last stockade more furiously than before, as they could see the little hut through the openings in the corral.

"Come in, uncles," shouted Stone boy. They obeyed him, and stepping to the center he said: "Watch me build my fence." Suiting the words, he took from his belt an arrow with a white stone fastened to the point and fastening it to his bow, he shot it high in the air. Straight up into the air it went, for two or three thousand feet, then seemed to stop suddenly and turned with point down and descended as swiftly as it had ascended. Upon striking the ground a high stone wall arose, enclosing the hut and all who were inside. Just then the buffalo broke the last stockade only to fill the last ditch up again. In vain did the leaders butt the stone wall. They hurt themselves, broke their horns and mashed their snouts, but could not even scar the wall.

The uncles and Stone boy in the meantime rained arrows of death into their ranks.

When the buffalo chief saw what they had to contend with, he ordered the fight off. The crier or herald sang out: "Come away, come away, Stone boy and his uncles will kill all of us."

So the buffalo withdrew, leaving over two thousand of their dead and wounded on the field, only to be skinned and put away for the feasts of Stone boy and his uncles, who lived to be great chiefs of their own tribe, and whose many relations soon joined them on the banks of Stone Boy Creek.

The Unktomi (Spider), Two Widows and the Red Plums

There once lived, in a remote part of a great forest, two widowed sisters, with their little babies. One day there came to their tent a visitor who was called Unktomi (spider). He had found some nice red plums during his wanderings in the forest, and he said to himself, "I will keep these plums and fool the two widows with them." After the widows had bidden him be seated, he presented them with the plums.

On seeing them they exclaimed "hi nu, hi nu (an exclamation of surprise), where did you get those fine plums?" Unktomi arose and pointing to a crimson tipped cloud, said: "You see that red cloud? Directly underneath it is a patch of plums. So large is the patch and so red and beautiful are the plums that it is the reflection of them on the cloud that you see."

"Oh, how we wish some one would take care of our babies, while we go over there and pick some," said the sisters. "Why, I am not in any particular hurry, so if you want to go I will take care of my little nephews until you return." (Unktomi always claimed relationship with everyone he met). "Well brother," said the older widow, "take good care of them and we will be back as soon as possible."

The two then took a sack in which to gather the plums, and started off towards the cloud with the crimson lining. Scarcely had they gone from Unktomi's sight when he took the babies out of their swinging hammocks and cut off first one head and then the other. He then took some old blankets and rolled them in the shape of a baby body and laid one in each hammock. Then he took the heads and put them in place in their different hammocks. The bodies he cut up and threw into a large kettle. This he placed over a rousing fire. Then he mixed Indian turnips and arikara squash with the baby meat and soon had a kettle of soup. Just about the time the soup was ready to serve the widows returned. They were tired and hungry and not a plum had they. Unktomi, hearing the approach of the two, hurriedly dished out the baby soup in two wooden dishes and then seated himself near the door so that he could get out easily. Upon the entrance of the widows, Unktomi exclaimed: "Sisters, I had brought some meat with me and I cooked some turnips and squash with it and made a pot of fine soup. The babies have just fallen asleep, so don't waken them until you have finished eating, for

I know that you are nearly starved." The two fell to at once and after they had somewhat appeased their appetites, one of them arose and went over to see how her baby was resting. Noting an unnatural color on her baby's face, she raised him up only to have his head roll off from the bundle of blankets. "'My son! my son!" she cried out. At once the other hastened to her baby and grabbed it up, only to have the same thing happen. At once they surmised who had done this, and caught up sticks from the fire with which to beat Unktomi to death. He, expecting something like this to happen, lost very little time in getting outside and down into a hole at the roots of a large tree. The two widows not being able to follow Unktomi down into the hole, had to give up trying to get him out, and passed the rest of the day and night crying for their beloved babies. In the meantime Unktomi had gotten out by another opening, and fixing himself up in an entirely different style, and painting his face in a manner that they would not recognize him, he cautiously approached the weeping women and inquired the cause of their tears.

Thus they answered him: "Unktomi came here and fooled us about some plums, and while we were absent killed our babies and made soup out of their bodies. Then he gave us the soup to eat, which we did, and when we found out what he had done we tried to kill him, but he crawled down into that hole and we could not get him out."

"I will get him out," said the mock stranger, and with that he crawled down into the hole and scratched his own face all over to make the widows believe he had been fighting with Unktomi. "I have killed him, and that you may see him I have enlarged the hole so you can crawl in and see for yourselves, also to take some revenge on his dead body." The two foolish widows, believing him, crawled into the hole, only to be blocked up by Unktomi, who at once gathered great piles of wood and stuffing it into the hole, set it on fire, and thus ended the last of the family who were foolish enough to let Unktomi tempt them with a few red plums.

A Note About the Author

Marie L. McLaughlin (1842–1933) was born in Minnesota and lived in a predominantly Native American community. She was educated at Prairie du Chien before marrying Major James McLaughlin in 1864. Her husband worked with an agency that helped to manage tribal affairs and enforce government policy. During his career, Marie was exposed to various indigenous cultures and in 1916, she wrote and published *Myths and Legends of the Sioux*. It's considered her most notable work and is comprised of many tales she learned throughout her life.

A Note from the Publisher

Spanning many genres, from non-fiction essays to literature classics to children's books and lyric poetry, Mint Edition books showcase the master works of our time in a modern new package. The text is freshly typeset, is clean and easy to read, and features a new note about the author in each volume. Many books also include exclusive new introductory material. Every book boasts a striking new cover, which makes it as appropriate for collecting as it is for gift giving. Mint Edition books are only printed when a reader orders them, so natural resources are not wasted. We're proud that our books are never manufactured in excess and exist only in the exact quantity they need to be read and enjoyed. To learn more and view our library, go to minteditionbooks.com

bookfinity & MINT EDITIONS

Enjoy more of your favorite classics with Bookfinity,
a new search and discovery experience for readers.
With Bookfinity, you can discover more vintage
literature for your collection, find your Reader Type,
track books you've read or want to read,
and add reviews to your favorite books.
Visit www.bookfinity.com, and click on
Take the Quiz to get started.

Don't forget to follow us
@bookfinityofficial and @mint_editions